RaumFragen: Stadt – Region – Landschaft

Series Editors

Olaf Kühne, Forschungsbereich Geographie, Eberhard Karls Universität Tübingen, Tübingen, Germany

Sebastian Kinder, Forschungsbereich Geographie, Eberhard Karls Universität Tübingen, Tübingen, Germany

Olaf Schnur, Stadt- und Quartiersforschung, Berlin, Germany

RaumFragen: Stadt – Region – Landschaft | SpaceAffairs: City – Region – Landscape

Im Zuge des „spatial turns" der Sozial- und Geisteswissenschaften hat sich die Zahl der wissenschaftlichen Forschungen in diesem Bereich deutlich erhöht. Mit der Reihe „RaumFragen: Stadt – Region – Landschaft" wird Wissenschaftlerinnen und Wissenschaftlern ein Forum angeboten, innovative Ansätze der Anthropogeographie und sozialwissenschaftlichen Raumforschung zu präsentieren. Die Reihe orientiert sich an grundsätzlichen Fragen des gesellschaftlichen Raumverständnisses. Dabei ist es das Ziel, unterschiedliche Theorieansätze der anthropogeographischen und sozialwissenschaftlichen Stadt- und Regionalforschung zu integrieren. Räumliche Bezüge sollen dabei insbesondere auf mikro- und mesoskaliger Ebene liegen. Die Reihe umfasst theoretische sowie theoriegeleitete empirische Arbeiten. Dazu gehören Monographien und Sammelbände, aber auch Einführungen in Teilaspekte der stadt- und regionalbezogenen geographischen und sozialwissenschaftlichen Forschung. Ergänzend werden auch Tagungsbände und Qualifikationsarbeiten (Dissertationen, Habilitationsschriften) publiziert.

In the course of the "spatial turn" of the social sciences and humanities, the number of scientific researches in this field has increased significantly. With the series "RaumFragen: Stadt – Region – Landschaft" scientists are offered a forum to present innovative approaches in anthropogeography and social space research. The series focuses on fundamental questions of the social understanding of space. The aim is to integrate different theoretical approaches of anthropogeographical and social-scientific urban and regional research. Spatial references should be on a micro- and mesoscale level in particular. The series comprises theoretical and theory-based empirical work. These include monographs and anthologies, but also introductions to some aspects of urban and regional geographical and social science research. In addition, conference proceedings and qualification papers (dissertations, postdoctoral theses) are also published.

More information about this series at http://www.springer.com/series/10584

Daniela Bernaschi

Collective Actions of Solidarity against Food Insecurity

The impact in terms of Capabilities

Springer VS

Daniela Bernaschi
University of Florence
Florence, Italy

This dissertation was accepted by the Department of Political and Social Sciences at the University of Florence and by the Department of Culture, Politics and Society at the University of Turin, in June 2019

ISSN 2625-6991 ISSN 2625-7009 (electronic)
RaumFragen: Stadt – Region – Landschaft
ISBN 978-3-658-31374-6 ISBN 978-3-658-31375-3 (eBook)
https://doi.org/10.1007/978-3-658-31375-3

Responsible Editor: Stefanie Eggert
This Springer VS imprint is published by the registered company Springer Fachmedien Wiesbaden GmbH part of Springer Nature.
The registered company address is: Abraham-Lincoln-Str. 46, 65189 Wiesbaden, Germany

*"Food security is one of the fundamental, global,
political and social challenges of our time.
We must innovate, at a local, national,
and international level, to create an enabling
food policy to fashion sustainable food economies
and end food insecurity and hunger".*

(Roberta Sonnino, 2018)

My deepest thanks to Prof. Jean-Michel Bonvin and Prof. Gianluca Brunori for their comments to my PhD thesis which this book is based on. A special thanks goes to my PhD supervisor Prof. Laura Leonardi for her ideas, comments, labor, mentorship and inspiration.

Acknowledgment

This book was made possible by the efforts and contributions of those who seek to collectively address the challenges posed by growing inequalities. My sincere gratitude goes to the coordinators of the Emporium of Solidarity in Rome, the Solidarity Card in Barcelona and the Solidarity Kitchen of the NGO Kipoda in Athens.

A special thanks is also due to the beneficiaries of these initiatives for their willingness to share their personal stories, despite the embarrassment of admitting they are deprived of the food security capability.

Food insecurity as the paradox of rich and opulent societies.

Introduction

The idea of hunger evokes in our collective imagination the places, situations and people that are far from the wealthy societies of the Northern World. This form of deprivation is singularly problematic. It is both geographical in nature, with the compass needle pointing towards the rural areas of developing countries, and also productivist, in that it is linked to the lack of food availability.

However, several empirical studies show a different scenario, in which food insecurity also affects cities, particularly the metropolises of rich societies (Dowler et al., 2011; Lambie-Mumford and Dowler, 2014; Sonnino, 2016). In these areas of the world, there is a clear contrast between opulence, the abundance of food resources (the root cause of the food waste issue), and a growing number of people who, because of job insecurity or inadequate wages and public social transfers, do not have access to the available market resources. Thus, we are witnessing the materialisation of what Campiglio and Rovati (2009) define as the paradox of "scarcity in abundance".

In Europe, for example, the economic crisis, rising unemployment and a policy of austerity (Sandbu, 2015; Perez and Matsaganis, 2018; Varoufakis, 2011) have had a significant impact on its citizens' living conditions. The impact is even more severe in Southern Europe (Duiella and Turrini, 2014; Cristancho and Loukakis, 2018). According to Eurostat data (2019), the number of people living in poverty and in conditions of social exclusion has increased, with 58 million people forced into a state of food insecurity. This situation has led to an increase in both the demand for food aid, and the number of food banks distributing cooked meals or food packages to people in need (Loopstra et al., 2015).

Thus, statistical surveys show that Europe is facing growing inequalities and that it is increasingly difficult to maintain all three terms of the Dahrendorf theorem (2009), namely economic efficiency, social cohesion and political freedoms. The urgency to react to the multiple forms of deprivation experienced by European citizens, has stimulated a response from local collective actions of solidarity. Collective actions of solidarity are collective civil society initiatives, with formal or informal organisational structures, that aim to meet the challenges triggered by economic difficulties and rising social inequalities, through alternative approaches. These initiatives are mainly implemented where there is an absence or shortage of public support for the most vulnerable social categories.

These collective actions are often examined in a philanthropic way, ignoring the impact they can have on the substantive freedoms of their beneficiaries and, more generally, on the root causes of poverty. These actions present a transformative and creative power and come in the form of food banks, community buying groups, alternative finance, free medical and legal assistance, etc. (Bosi and Zamponi, 2015; Kousis, 2017, Kousis and Paschou, 2017; Papadaki and Kalogeraki, 2018).

This book analyses the issue of food insecurity in Europe, highlighting the role played by collective actions of solidarity in promoting resilient, solidarity-based and food-safe communities. The aim of the research is to understand whether these collective initiatives are *capability-oriented* or merely *compensating for shortcomings*, and also to determine what contributions can be made to the definition of a new food policy "by" and "for" cities.

Indeed, food insecurity in urban areas -particularly in developed countries- is a poorly understood phenomenon. Food security interventions have primarily focused on ensuring food availability, which has led to predominantly *production-oriented* responses that presuppose a rural challenge, overlooking urban food insecurity challenges.

This book draws on the original analysis of emerging local food security actions, highlighting how a food lens can offer opportunities to explore innovative forms of urban governance, participatory planning and citizen-driven food policies, with their impact in terms of capabilities.

Urban food insecurity and its related consequences raise questions about the role of cities in the food system and the active role played by collective actions of solidarity and local public institutions. These questions provided momentum to the research field in three European countries: Italy, Spain and Greece. This book will present the results of an empirical study, starting in October 2016 and ending in June 2019, with the aim of analysing -in comparative terms- three different initiatives in Rome, Barcelona and Athens, in order to address their impact on the fight against food insecurity.

The research is based on primary data collected through interviews with key informants, participant observation and in-depth semi-structured interviews with both the beneficiaries and the coordinators of the collective actions of solidarity. In total, 110 qualitative interviews were carried out. The focus of the interviews with the beneficiaries is not on what people "do" or "are". On the contrary, through a longitudinal analysis (supported by the Nvivo software) and the reconstruction of their life paths, the aim is to understand what people are "free to do and to be", and how the collective actions of solidarity affect their substantive freedoms.

The collective initiatives investigated are: the "Emporium of Solidarity" of Caritas in Rome, the "Solidarity Card" promoted by Caritas and the Municipality of Barcelona, and finally, the "Solidarity Kitchen" of the NGO Kipoda in Athens.

This work is divided into eight chapters. The first will address the problem of food insecurity in Europe, with the aim of elaborating a definition that can better identify the multidimensional and dynamic nature of the issue. This will go beyond the mere availability of food, in order to encompass the cross-cutting issues of the disconnect between food production and the human condition of food security.

The second chapter will focus on the dual concept of food and cities and the increasing involvement of collective initiatives in developing innovative responses to food insecurity and poverty challenges. Thanks to certain initiatives in Rome, Barcelona and Athens, the role played by local dimension and how it relates to the global dimension through networks, agreements and shared knowledges, will be highlighted.

The third chapter will explore the contribution of the capability approach by the economist and Nobel Prize winner Amartya Sen, to understanding the impact of collective actions of solidarity in terms of strengthening substantive freedoms. A definition of solidarity in terms of social co-responsibility will be defined. Indeed, poverty, environmental sustainability and food insecurity, are social challenges that increasingly need to be addressed through participation-based approaches.

In the fourth chapter, the methodologies used will be clearly defined, and a proposal for the operationalisation of the capability approach will be outlined. Then, a general definition will be given of *capability-oriented* initiatives and mere *compensation for shortcomings* initiatives: what they are and how they can be distinguished.

The fifth and sixth chapters present the results of the empirical research, with a focus on the Emporium of Solidarity, the Solidarity Card and the Solidarity Kitchen. The book aims to understand the nature of these initiatives and their impact in terms of strengthening the beneficiaries' agency and capabilities, on one hand, and on the other hand, in terms of empowering the capability for voice of those who, owing to a lack of rights and resources, have no voice.

In chapter seven, a study of the empirical data will enable to distinguish collective actions of solidarity that are *capabilities-oriented* from those that merely aim to compensate for shortcomings. The socio-institutional contexts affecting the collective actions will be investigated.

And lastly, in the final remarks, the crucial role played by the *capabilities-oriented* approach in tackling food insecurity, and the impact of city-based collective actions of solidarity will be discussed. This discussion will take place alongside an analysis of the policy implications, in the light of the environmental and social sustainability embedded in the food security concept.

Contents

1 Food Insecurity in Europe: From the Availability of Food to the Substantive Freedoms in Accessing it

1.1 The Measure of Food Insecurity, from Protein Meals to the Quality of Nutrition: A Focus on Italy, Spain and Greece

In 2008, the economic crisis overwhelmed Europe and severely hit employment, the production system and human security (Sen, 2012; Scott, 2007). The consequences of the economic crisis were felt to varying intensities in different European countries and were more severe in Southern Europe (Duiella and Turrini, 2014; Cristancho and Loukakis, 2018), where the recession was exacerbated by the pernicious effects of austerity policies.

The rise in unemployment, the Neet rate[1] and job insecurity, alongside a fall in incomes and the non-economic effects of vulnerability, had a significant impact on the living conditions of European citizens. These led to an increase in poverty, social exclusion and the number of people living in a state of food insecurity (Matsaganis and Leventi, 2014).

The officially accepted definition of food security is the one developed by the World Food Summit (1996). It describes food security as a situation in which: "*All people, at all times, have physical, social and economic access to sufficient, safe and nutritious food which meets their dietary needs and food preferences for an active and healthy life*".

[1]Not in Education, Employment or Training (NEET) are young people -in the 15–29 age group- who are not in education, employment or training.

D. Bernaschi, *Collective Actions of Solidarity against Food Insecurity*, RaumFragen: Stadt – Region – Landschaft, https://doi.org/10.1007/978-3-658-31375-3_1

At the European level, food insecurity is measured by a specific indicator[2] (an integral part of a set of indicators that define the risk of poverty and social exclusion), which assesses the ability of households to afford a meal based on "meat, fish or the vegetarian equivalent", every two days. According to Eurostat (2019), 11.3% and, therefore, almost 58 million people in Europe cannot afford a protein meal every two days.

Bulgaria has the highest percentage with 43.8% (2018), but decreasing from 65.2% in 2013. In Mediterranean countries, as we can see in the graph in Figure 1.1 (p. 5), food deprivation is more severe in Italy, where, in 2018, 16% could not afford a protein meal, while in Greece it was 13.1%. In both cases, this was an increase compared to the 2015 data, where deprivation was 10.8% in Greece and 14.3% in Italy. Looking at the trend from 2015 to 2018, both Italy and Greece show higher percentages than the European average. In 2018, the European Union (EU-28) saw a decrease in food insecurity to 11.3% down from 12.4% in 2015. Nevertheless, although below the European average, Spain had the largest increase from 3.9% in 2015 to 6.2% in 2018. The number of people who cannot afford a protein meal every two days has therefore nearly doubled.

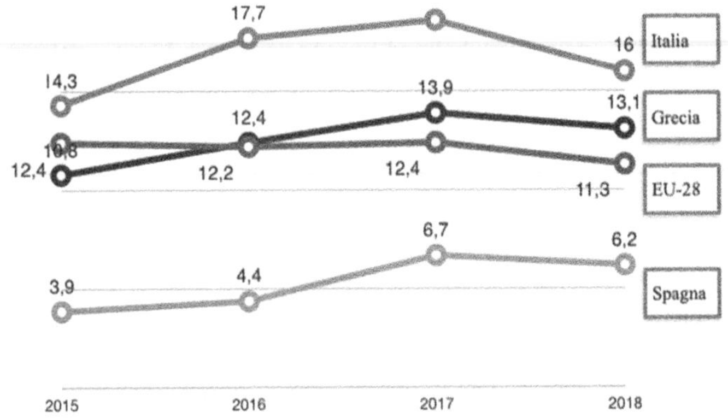

Figure 1.1 Inability to afford a protein meal or vegetarian equivalent every second day. *Source* Author's elaboration based on Eurostat data (2019)

[2]A person is at risk of poverty if he or she is in one of the following three conditions:

The risk of poverty: this is a measure of relative poverty after social transfers, taxes and other deductions. It assesses the number of people whose household income is below the at-risk-of-poverty threshold set at 60% of the national median.

Condition of severe deprivation: when people find it difficult to meet at least four from a list of nine needs and services: paying rent or bills on time; adequately heating the home; facing unforeseen expenses; eating meat, fish or the vegetarian equivalent every other day; a week's holiday; a car; a washing machine; a colour TV or a telephone (including a mobile phone).

Belonging to families with very low work intensity: people aged 0–59 years living in households where, on average, adults (18–59) have worked less than 20% of their work potential in the last year. Students are excluded.

Integrating the Eurostat report with the FAO survey (2013), the "Food Insecurity Experience Scale"[3] indicator shows that in Spain, 12% of children aged under 15 live in a state of food insecurity. The situation does not improve in Greece (15.7%), and while in Italy we find a lower figure (8.8%), it is no less worrying.

An interesting aspect to highlight is that food insecurity does not simply mean lack of access to food, but the condition of poverty can also lead to a state of malnutrition. In fact, the need to reduce budget expenditure not only reduces the consumption of food, but also leads to low quality nutrition (Marques-Vidal et al., 2015). Thus, the answer to Dietz's question (1995) "Can hunger cause obesity?" turns out, in some cases, to be "yes".

In fact, according to UNICEF (2017), in the 2014–2015 period, 18% of children aged between 11 and 15 in Italy, 20.9% in Greece and 17.3% in Spain were obese or overweight. Children seem to be among the main victims of a deprived social context. In reaction, programmes have been introduced in public school cafeterias, to ensure a balanced and high-quality diet. Examples of these are scholarships promoted by local public institutions, such as the Municipality of Barcelona with the "Becas de Comedor" (Food Grants) programme, or by shipowners' foundations such as the "Stavros Niarchos Foundation" in Greece with its "Food Aid and Promotion of Healthy Nutrition" programme.

1.2 From an Emergency Approach to a Substantive Freedoms Approach to Food Security

The main surveys show how fragile it is to link the problem of food insecurity *exclusively* to the level of economic development, while restricting the boundaries of its geography to the rural areas of developing countries. Indeed, there is another highly contrasting scenario in which food insecurity also affects rich industrialised countries (Dowler et al., 2011; Lambie-Mumford and Dowler, 2014; Sonnino, 2016), where there is an increase in both the demand for food aid and the number of active food banks (Loopstra et al., 2015). The social categories[4] most affected by this problem are women, children aged under 15, and people over 65 years old (European Commission, 2015).

[3]Indicator developed under the "Voices of the Hungry" project and implemented to track achievement of the United Nations Millennium Development Goals (MDGs). Food insecurity is defined as a situation where there is no secure access to a quantity of food that meets people's nutritional and cultural needs.

[4]According to the summary report of the European Commission (2015) on the results of the implementation of FEAD (Fund for European Aid to the Most Deprived), of the 11 million beneficiaries, 51% are women, followed by 3 million young people aged under 15 and 1.2 million people aged over 65. Among the beneficiaries we also find:

719,708 migrants, including refugees and children;
621,979 people with disabilities; and
69,451 homeless people.

While on the one hand, there is an abundance of food production from which the problem of food waste originates[5] (European Commission, 2010), on the other hand, there is a growing number of people who are unable to access the available food resources, owing to a lack of employment or insufficient income and public transfers. Therefore, there is a conflict between the resources available on the market and rights of access to them. This conflict often finds its solution in the redistribution of surpluses from production system.

In fact, in some European countries, the lack of a national legal framework to guarantee the right to food (missing from the constitutions of European countries[6]) and provide adequate forms of income support for the most vulnerable social groups,[7] has led to the prevalence of an approach built on availability and, hence, on food supply. Consequently, the focus on the "availability" of food is reflected both in a European indicator that evaluates the "number" of meals received, highlighting the "quantitative" nature of deprivation, and in policies oriented towards the distribution of European agricultural surpluses and large-scale distribution surplus to charities.[8]

The European commitment to tackling food insecurity was started back in 1987, when Jacques Delors, at that time, the President of the European Commission, established the Food Distribution Programme for the Most Deprived Persons (PEAD) under the Common Agricultural Policy (CAP). The PEAD distributed agricultural surpluses, stored during periods in which production exceeded Community demand (and supplemented with purchases made on the market in the mid-1990s), to countries wishing to provide food aid for the most deprived. This programme was a fundamental means of supply for all charitable organisations around Europe (Frigo 2015).

[5]Food waste arises when surpluses from the production system (those goods that are produced, processed and distributed by the supply chain and for various reasons are not sold and, therefore, consumed), are not used either for social purposes (e.g. donations to charities) or environmental purposes, for example, for animal feed or for the production of goods and energy (Maino et al., 2016, p. 35).

[6]The right to food is only recognised internationally with the Universal Declaration of Human Rights (Article 25, 1948) and the International Covenant on Economic, Social and Cultural Rights of 1966 (Article 11.2a). Only in countries where hunger is a political and social problem do the more recent Constitutional Covenants constitutionalise the right to food as in: Bolivia (Article 16), Brazil (Articles 6 and 7), Ecuador (Article 13), South Africa (Article 27).

[7]As pointed out by Gramaglia and Bolzoni (2016), minimum income schemes could play a crucial role in the fight against growing inequalities, only when their inclusive nature prevails and, therefore, universality of access is guaranteed. Moreover, the low level of generosity and stringent access requirements that often characterize these measures may substantially limit their protective effect (Frazer and Marlier, 2016).

[8]Consider the recent Italian legislation: food donations by companies are made possible by a particular legislative framework that encourages them with tax reductions (Good Samaritan Law of 2003, and Law No. 166 of 19 August 2016).

In February 2014, PEAD was replaced by the Fund for European Aid to the Most Deprived (FEAD). This transition is linked not only to the unpredictability of stocks and their possible collapse due to the reforms of the CAP (Ibid. 2015), but also to the need to adopt wide-ranging measures aimed at countering an extremely critical situation which, in 2014, saw almost 50 million people experience a state of severe material deprivation, within the borders of flourishing EU nations. This means that 8.9% of people in Europe did not have enough money to heat their homes, afford a protein meal or meet unforeseen expenses.

In general, it arises the adoption of an "emergency" approach rather than a "structural" one to food insecurity. This approach does not take account of the entitlements that define food insecurity, and instead, creates a questionable interdependence with the issues of food waste. Indeed, the focus seems to be only on food resources distribution.

As the Stiglitz-Sen-Fitoussi report[9] observes "*what we measure affects what we do and if our measurements are inflated, decisions may be distorted*" (Stiglitz et al., 2009, p. 7). The measure devised by Eurostat provides information on the dimension taken by food deprivation (Davis and Baumberg 2016), focusing on food use, which is unlike other measures that are more subjective (Lambie-Mumford et al. 2014; Coleman-Jensen et al. 2012; Dowler 2002).

At the same time, as Davis and Baumberg (2016) point out, it only focuses on one dimension of food security, namely the quantities consumed. In fact, it does not take into account other crucial aspects such as nutritional deficiencies, anxiety about food self-sufficiency and social stigmas. All of which, are only taken into consideration in measures such as the Radimer/Cornell hunger scale, but not in transnational surveys (Ibidem, 2016).

Indeed, food insecurity not only concerns the lack of access to a quantity of food necessary for one's survival, but implies an absence of autonomy and control over one's own food with its crucial social and relational impacts. Therefore, it is worthwhile to include the analysis of food insecurity within a broader study on social exclusion, in terms of deprivation of substantive freedoms (Sen 2000; Salais 2009).

Social exclusion plays both a "constitutive" role and an "instrumental" role in limiting people's substantive freedoms. It is constitutive, because the impossibility of freely interacting with others, of not being and feeling part of the community, is already an important deprivation that can contribute to an impoverishment of life itself (Salais, 2009). For example, we can consider the effects of a state of food insecurity: anxiety about the lack of autonomy in finding food, shame, social stigma, humiliation and the consequent social isolation. Social exclusion also plays an instrumental role. Being excluded from the labour market, for example, and not having secure and decent paid employment can

---

[9]Inquiry Committee set up in 2008 following a proposal by the French Government. The work underlined the importance of an alternative measure to GDP for assessing a nation's level of well-being and social progress.

lead to other forms of deprivation in terms of food, health and housing conditions. All of which have significant impacts on social relationships.

Thus, social exclusion and food insecurity reinforce each other through a multiplicative process of deprivation, and this gives food insecurity a multidimensional and dynamic component that goes beyond the mere availability of food. As a consequence, both the indicators and the related programmes to tackle food insecurity, need to shift from an emergency approach based on the distribution of food, to a substantive freedoms approach. This new approach should address the precipitating conditions leading to a state of food insecurity.

1.3 The Precipitating Factors of a State of Food Insecurity: Availability, Access and Social use of Food

Food security holds deep socio-economic roots. As Holt Giménez and Shattuck (2011) observe, in 2008, food riots took place in cities where food was available but many could not afford it. Indeed, food prices were too high and prevented the poorest from being able to buy it (Mendes and Sonnino 2018). Therefore, it is crucial to combine an analytical perspective that is solely agricultural/productivist, with one that aims to deepen the social "precipitating" and "characterising" conditions of food insecurity. The attention should move from "farmland" to a systemic approach that also considers "actual access" to food and its social and policy implications.

"*The notion of food security has an important history as a key concept for 20th-century policymakers. Two overarching perspectives on food security are identified. One centered on raising production as the core answer to under-consumption and hunger. The other is an emerging perspective, more social and ecological, accepting the need to address a complex array of problems, not just production*" (Lang and Barling 2012, p. 313).

In the literature on food insecurity and the programmes to tackle it, the work of the Indian economist and philosopher Amartya Sen has played a pioneering role in breaking the prevailing productivity paradigm of the 1980s. His work challenged the close correlation between reducing hunger and increasing agricultural productivity.

In a popular work by Sen from 1981, "Poverty and Famines", the issues of famine and hunger[10] are instead explained by looking at those economic and political changes that can deprive some social groups—the most vulnerable—of the entitlements needed to access food. These entitlements are actual property rights over food that people can enjoy (Sen, 1997). Sen defines them as: "*The set of alternative commodity bundles that a*

[10]Dreze and Sen (1989, p. 7) make a distinction between the issues of famine and hunger, defining the former as "*acute starvation and a sharp increase of mortality*", and the latter as a condition of "*sustained nutritional deprivation on a persistent basis*".

person can command in a society using the totality of rights and opportunities that he or she faces" (1984, p. 497).

Entitlements are essentially affected by two elements:

- the personal endowments and, therefore, the resources that a person legally owns, e.g. a house, a land to cultivate, livestock and non-tangible assets (Osmani, 1995); and
- the set of goods that Sen defines as "*exchange entitlement mapping*" (Sen, 1981, p. 435), which a person can access through the market and the production system.

A decline in endowments or in the price of the goods a person produces, can reduce his or her ability to purchase food. Therefore, the role of public policies in supporting entitlements through opportune anti-poverty programmes is crucial. In India, for example, after Independence in 1947, it was possible to prevent the risk of famine through the creation of emergency public works to reconstitute the lost entitlements of people in a more vulnerable situation[11] (Sen, 2000).

As a result, rights and resources are linked and interdependent but in an unstable way. Indeed, in a market economy, they are affected not only by our resources (i.e. our labour force, land and other production factors that we can use or that we can sell), but also by price trends for what we sell and the goods we intend to purchase. Moreover, they are strongly influenced by non-economic institutions that are part of the framework of opportunities (such as, family and associations).

By studying the famines in Bengal (1943), Ethiopia (1973) and Bangladesh (1974), Amartya Sen highlighted the socio-economic conditions (unemployment and increase in the price of certain goods, such as rice), which explain the increase in the mortality rate in the most vulnerable social groups. As Osmani (1995) points out, Sen does not question the importance of the availability of food resources, but rather, he calls into question an approach that aims to explain famine by rigidly observing only that dimension.

According to Dreze and Sen (1989), if people experience hunger on a regular or seasonal basis, the reasons must be traced to the way the existing entitlements system fails to provide people with sufficient means to acquire enough food. Seeing hunger as a failure of the broader system of entitlements, above and beyond food availability, allows us to understand the driving forces of hunger and identify the relevant actions to contrast it.

Amartya Sen's research has played a pivotal role in broadening the horizons of food security literature, by shifting the focus from the "availability" of food, to "access" and actual "use" of food. In doing so, he has highlighted the personal, social and relational

---

[11]According to Sen (1999), these measures have a limited impact on the state budget because the potential "victims" of famine represent 5–10% of the total population.

conversion factors[12] involved in converting a certain endowment of resources into effective freedoms.

From this perspective, the aim is not to provide a particular amount of food for each person. Dreze and Sen (1989) point out that the relationship between food intake and the related nutritional achievements depend not only on characteristics such as age, gender, potential pregnancy status and climatic conditions, but also on the access to complementary inputs. Complementary inputs such as the availability of drinking water, health services, basic education, epidemic prevention programmes, generally affect the conversion of food into the substantive freedom to be well-nourished.

Additionally, the use of food draws attention to a key aspect of food security, which concerns "food safety", namely the hygienic and sanitary conditions of food production systems and the way food is processed and cooked. Healthy agro-ecosystems are crucial for their impact on people's health and therefore on their well-being. In this regard, the recent COVID-19 pandemic[13] emerges as a clear example.

---

[12]Sen highlights (1999, p. 70–71, 1987a) five main sources which affect the conversion of resources into freedom:

Personal heterogeneity: human beings differ greatly in their physical characteristics related to age, gender, presence or absence of any disease. For example, a person with health issues may need a higher income for health care than a healthy person.

Environmental diversity: the presence of contagious diseases (malaria, AIDS), water and air contamination, profoundly alter people's quality of life.

Diversity in the social context: the transformation of resources into capabilities is also influenced by social conditions such as social capital (relations with the community), the absence or presence of crime, public health care and education.

Relative differences: in a rich society, a person needs goods and resources to participate in the life of the community that are not needed in a poor society. Moreover, one may be poor in a rich society, despite the fact that income, in absolute terms, is greater than what might be needed in a poorer community.

Distribution within the family: the well-being and freedoms of family members are determined by the way the family's income is used to promote everyone's capabilities. Referring to an empirical study in Ivory Coast, Philippines and Gambia, Gustav Ranis et al. (2000) highlight that the education of women and their control over their own income lead to a more equitable distribution of resources between male and female children and a greater disposition to invest in health, nutrition and education.

[13]COVID-19 is a respiratory disease caused by the SARS-CoV-2 coronavirus, which resulted in a pandemic beginning in December 2019 in the city of Wuhan, capital of China's Hubei Province, and later spreading throughout the world.

The first cases mainly involved workers in Wuhan's "wet market" where wild animals were sold. In these markets, there is a higher risk of viruses being transmitted from animals to humans, due to the difficulty maintaining hygiene standards in an environment where live animals, often caged with other animal species, are slaughtered on site. The source of COVID-19 has not yet been traced, but it is thought to be a bat that may have infected other animals sold at the market.

Enhancing the social and institutional dimensions of food deprivation allows us to combine an analysis of the "access" to food, with one on the "use" of food. The conditions of access to food leads to an analysis of entitlements, that is, the set of rights and opportunities available to people (Sen, 1981).

At the same time, a study on nutritional, social, relational and convivial needs (Illich, 1972; Levi-Strauss, 1966; Bourdieu, 1979), linked to a safe use of food (Dreze and Sen, 1989), allows us to look at food insecurity not only as a condition of nutritional deficiency, but also as a lack of autonomy and control over one's own diet. Thus, it affects the substantive freedom to feel and take an active part in the life of the community without feeling ashamed (Smith, 1759).

Receiving food parcels from charitable organisations or going to soup kitchens diminishes freedom of choice regarding the quality and diversity of one's diet (FAO, 2019), and in terms of the ability to meet nutritional, social and convivial needs. The concept of "conviviality" stems from the Latin "*convivium*" and "*convivère*", meaning "living together". Therefore, if the food-sharing dimension is absent, what is missing is an idea of food that goes beyond nourishment and becomes an opportunity for dialogue and reflection (Illich, 1972). The distribution of standardised products is part of an emergency approach aimed at "feeding" people, without recognising human diversity and the different social and individual conversion factors. This leads to a myopic viewpoint that does not affect the structural conditions of a state of food deprivation.

With these considerations as premises, a study on food security that leverages its multidimensionality seems to be an important undertaking. In other words, as shown in Figure 1.2 (p. 11) the condition of food security can be described as a dynamic flow that leads from entitlements (one's own food production; income from selling one's own production; and income from employment) affected by welfare policies (e.g. income integration policies) and personal and social conversion factors (personal skills; presence of an enabling or disabling social context in terms of freedoms) to a particular mechanism for accessing food. A mechanism that is influenced by market trends and prices.

In more detail, individual and social conversion factors, on the one hand, turn the entitlements into the freedom to choose between a different combination of food items that meet one's personal nutritional, social and convivial needs. That is, they become substantive food-related freedoms. On the other hand, they convert food-related freedoms into an actual achievement, that of being "food-secure" in its broadest definition, which includes the availability, the "access to" and the use of food. Hence, a holistic approach must be implemented in order to address the cross-cutting issues of the disconnect between food production and the state of food security.

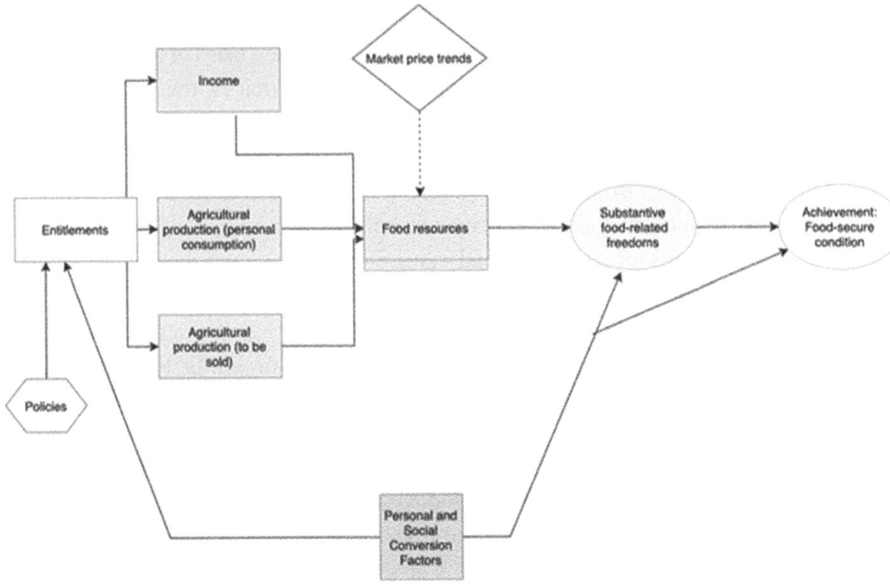

Figure 1.2 Food security: from entitlements, substantive food-related freedoms, to the condition of food security. *Source* Author's elaboration

2 Collective Initiatives and Their Innovative Responses to Food Insecurity Challenges

2.1 Urban Food Diplomacy: The Local Dimension of Food Security from a Global Impact Perspective

In the context of *glocalisation* (Bauman, 2005), the local dimension as the ongoing setting for fundamental human action (Appadurai, 2014) turns the spotlight on the role played by cities at political, financial and resource displacement levels[1] (Sassen, 2003, 2016), as well as on the incubation of initiatives with a strong innovative value and global influence (Schwan, 2017).

The close link between food and cities appears when we consider that almost half of the world's population lives in cities, and the urban systems of supply, production and consumption are crucial for the impact they can have on the problems of hunger, rural poverty and climate change.

Cities are facing the challenging issue of handling and controlling the food supply system (Marsden and Sonnino, 2008, 2012). A sustainable system that allows and maintains the "feeding" of a growing population in the context of environmental and human sustainability. There is a strong need for a greening of food security (Duncan, 2015), i.e. "*the introduction or reformulation of policies, practices, products and/or processes in order to address key environmental issues*" (Crane, 2000, p. 674). Issues such as the consumption patterns that have a strong impact on natural resources, or the increasing

[1] According to Bagnasco et al. (2001, p. 236), we should not be surprised if globalization and the process by which the European Union was built, have led to cities with increased power taking decisive political action. Cities often pursue their own foreign policy and promote legislative initiatives in European Union authorities, establishing alliances with each other and promoting their economic identity.

D. Bernaschi, *Collective Actions of Solidarity against Food Insecurity*, RaumFragen: Stadt – Region – Landschaft, https://doi.org/10.1007/978-3-658-31375-3_2

depletion of fertile land (due to the intensification of production and the widespread use of pesticides).

According to Marsden (2013), production systems are not sustainable because they are based on a reckless use of environmental and social resources, that are subject to progressive deterioration. Therefore, the issue of "food resource availability" emerges as a strategic area through which to ensure social order.

In this regard, the dual concept of food and city has strong historical roots. Charles Tilly (1975) points out that control over food has also been decisive in the constitution of States, in order to overcome systems where resources were managed strictly by agricultural communities. Over time, food supply has also become a public order issue. It is worth mentioning the San Martino bread riots (1628), the Flour War (1775), the riots of agricultural and industrial labourers in East Anglia (1816), and even the 2010 bread riots in Tunisia and in other Northern African countries which, to a certain extent, marked the beginning of the "Arab Spring" (Sonnino, 2018).

The powerful relationship between cities and the issue of food has been further strengthened thanks to the Millennium Development Goals drawn up in 2015 by the United Nations. Indeed, there is an international commitment in the fight against hunger to achieve food security through sustainable agriculture. At the same time, the importance of making cities inclusive, safe, resilient and sustainable is also highlighted.

Global issues and the local dimension are therefore interconnected, triggering what some have called "Urban Food Diplomacy" (Mann, 2019); a diplomacy designed to strengthen the collaborative network between cities around the world, with all cooperating for a sustainable and resilient transition of urban areas.

This diplomacy (BCFN and MUFPP, 2018) can be found in a number of projects at the European and international levels, such as FAO's "Food in cities" initiative to facilitate an international networking system; the Eurocities Network, which brings together local governments from over 140 European cities, representing them in the European Institutions and facilitating the exchange of good practices between the various social actors.

Another is the C40 Cities Climate Leadership Group initiative, which is an important network of the world's major cities and works to tackle the risks of climate change; and the 100 Resilient Cities that is a Rockefeller Foundations project, which supports cities in facing the main social and environmental challenges, creating resilient environments for their inhabitants.

And finally, another project that should be mentioned is the Ellen MacArthur Foundation initiative that links cities to circular economy projects, in order to encourage a transition from urban food systems that cause pollution and waste resources, to more sustainable ones. This transition is possible through collective and shared social action between public institutions and civil society.

The local dimension also takes on a global role under the Milan Urban Food Policy Pact (2015), which has been signed by over 160 cities around the world. The pact commits city mayors to working on building a sustainable food system, guaranteeing healthy and accessible food for all, preserving biodiversity and reducing food waste.

Considering all these initiatives, the international engagement that emerges drives cities towards a more concrete commitment. For example, the Municipality of Barcelona has adopted the food strategy "*l'Estratègia d'Impuls de la Política Alimentària 2016–2019*", which states that food security must be tackled from a multidimensional perspective, targeting food sovereignty,[2] sustainable consumption, agro-ecological production, enhancing local production and reducing food waste. This strategy follows the signing of the Milan Urban Food Policy Pact (2015) and the Charter for Food Sovereignty drawn up in Zaragoza in 2014 (during the first International Congress of Social and Solidarity Economics), which highlights the leading role of municipalities in the development of sustainable food policies.

The leading role of local initiatives is also highlighted by the project "*A food policy for Rome*" promoted by two collective actions of solidarity: *Terra!* and *Lands Onlus*. A participatory process, involving more than fifty organisations and researchers, has led to the drawing up of a proposal to be submitted to the public institutions. A food policy to support local producers, empower the short supply chain (farmers' markets; community buying groups), solidarity-based economies, and guarantee the right of all to sustainable and high-quality food.

Therefore, cities seem to be strategic platforms on which start developing food security policies, as they are places where social marginalisation and inequalities are more visible (Sonnino, 2016, 2018). In fact, the emerging literature emphasises the potential role they can play in the definition of sustainable and inclusive food policies, by focusing on trans-local collective actions and maintaining synergy with local public institutions (Bauman, 2005; Appadurai, 2014).

The local schemes undertaken by collective initiatives and local public institutions vitalise city life, and do not merely capture the socio-economic change occurring, adapting their counteraction (Simiti, 2017; Kousis, 2016). On the contrary, they also aim to strengthen democratic participation, by expanding individual and collective agency and contributing to social change in regard to substantive freedoms. According to Gascon and Montagut (2015), the dominant economic-productive framework causes more and more poverty and inequality, and is clearly unsustainable. Therefore, transforming this paradigm must be a priority, by promoting local development strategies that contribute to generating and redistributing wealth and reinforcing people's well-being.

2.2 Collective Initiatives in Italy, Spain and Greece

The literature highlights the relationship between the economic crisis and the rise in the number of initiatives aimed at "collectively" addressing the increase in poverty and food insecurity (Papadaki and Kalogeraki, 2018; D'Alisa et al., 2015; Kousis et al., 2016).

[2]Food sovereignty means "*the right of peoples to healthy and culturally appropriate food produced through ecologically sound and sustainable methods, and their right to define their own food and agricultural systems*" (Nyéléni Declaration, Mali, Forum on Food Sovereignty, 2007).

Crisis and austerity measures have produced different effects that vary according to the formal or informal nature of the initiatives (Simiti, 2015). Regarding initiatives with formal arrangements, the 2008–2010 period saw deep changes to their budgets, because private donors, foundations and governments significantly reduced their economic support (Hanfstaengl, 2010). As a result of this, initiatives were forced to reduce their activities and their staff. This is confirmed in a study conducted by Shahin et al. (2013) on the effects of the economic crisis on collective actions in Europe. This crisis would also deepen the gap between small and large formal organisations.

Moreover, owing to cuts in social expenditure in Southern European Countries, organisations that are traditionally dependent on government support, have been forced to expand their collaborative networks and seek economic support from European funds (Simiti, 2015). The economic crisis, therefore, has had a twofold impact on collective initiatives. First, it has revitalised formal (e.g. NGOs) and informal associations in the form of solidarity networks and help groups (Huliarias, 2015; Sotiropoulos and Bourikos, 2014; Kousis, 2017).

Second, as a consequence of austerity policies, it has encouraged formal organisations to look for funding at the European level, freeing them from their reliance on national governments. For example, as a result of the crisis, the non-profit world in Greece underwent a shift away from public financial support to being backed by foundations. Philanthropic foundations, such as shipowners' foundations, play a crucial role in supporting collective initiatives and also in developing researches with social purposes.[3]

As Kantzara (2014) points out, the economic crisis has severely challenged traditional anti-poverty programmes and has stimulated the involvement of different social actors (municipalities, private foundations, cooperatives, organisations, informal networks, trade unions, businesses, and the Catholic and Orthodox Churches) in the development of new welfare structures: solidarity pharmacies, solidarity supermarkets, urban gardens and self-managed social soup kitchens.[4]

---

[3]In 2013, for example, the Stavros Niarchos Foundation, collaborating with a research group led by Professor Salome Papaspyrou Rao of Rutgers University (New Jersey, USA), wrote the first study on food insecurity in Greece. Stavros Niarchos also organises the distribution of free meals in schools in order to address the issue of child food insecurity.

[4]For example, in Athens, the Municipality's "Kyada" scheme, a soup kitchen that distributes daily meals to migrants, homeless people and drug addicts, is provisioned by Apostolì, an NGO of the Orthodox Church. Apostolì has a complex structure:

a) it supplies municipal canteens in Athens with prepared meals;

b) it has its own soup kitchen;

it distributes food parcels; and

c) it helps about 4000 families, providing credit cards that people can only use to purchase fresh produce.

d) Considering that canteens and parcels cannot be the real answer to poverty, Apostolì provides financial support to agricultural cooperatives in Northern Greece.

What emerges, therefore, is a strengthening of both horizontal cooperation between the various associations, and also vertical cooperation with the local governments which provide a range of services, using municipal buildings, such as social clinics with volunteer doctors. In Italy, Spain and Greece, collective initiatives have highlighted how the local dimension is able to react with alternative solutions to the problem of food deprivation, to the growing inequalities increasingly affect economically developed societies (see the information box, p. 17).

The economic crisis has not only generated, in some social contexts, a deeper collaboration between collective actions and local governments, but it has also fostered new forms of participation characterized by informal organisational structures and a strong "anti-state/anti-European" orientation. These initiatives tend to be politicised in nature, which leads them to consider central governments and the EU as the main contributors to the current state of crisis, leading them to prefer being supported by local institutions.

The role of collective initiatives and local governments and, therefore, the "local" dimension of development has emerged strongly thanks to the influence of the social movements which followed the path set by the *Indignados* in Spain. According to these movements, indignation had to be transformed into concrete action at local level. This led to the emergence of collective initiatives with strong local roots, and a dense network of relationships and communication with other initiatives in the area. It also revealed the importance of establishing a collaborative relationship, designed "on a local scale" with local governments.

As some empirical studies show (Lahusen and Loukakis, 2016), the 2008 economic crisis and the influence of social movements seem to have given a boost to and strengthened alternative methods of participation (Simiti, 2017; Rakopoulos, 2014, 2016; Pautz and Kominou, 2012; Petropoulou, 2013; Sotiropoulos, 2014). The countries with the highest percentage of new initiatives are those that were most affected by the crisis. For example, more than half of the initiatives in Greece[5] (56.2%) and Spain (50.4%) were started after 2008 (Lahusen and Loukakis, 2016).

Of the more than 4000 initiatives analysed by the European research project LIVEWHAT[6] (2016), 52.7% address basic needs (distribution of food and clothing, housing support for the homeless, medical services, free legal support, anti-fraud

[5]In post-dictatorship Greece, civil society was "weak", owing to the strong role of the State and the control of political parties over the civic sector which turned into powerful cronyism-based networks (Sotiropoulos, 2014; Mouzelis, 1995). With the economic crisis, however, it has strengthened its autonomy from the parties and the State (Simiti, 2017).

[6]"*LIVEWHAT FP7 Living with Hard Times How Citizens React to Economic Crises and Their Social and Political Consequences*" is based on the analysis of 1,297 European initiatives randomly selected. The research was divided into three distinct stages:

1. analysis of websites;
2. online survey for coordinators; and
3. qualitative interviews with members of the initiatives.

initiatives and aid groups for women, children and refugees), 46% are involved in cultural activities and public awareness and, lastly, 42.6% are engaged in alternative economic activities (alternative currencies, barter systems, distribution systems of low-cost goods and services).

In Italy, activities related to alternative consumption are the most frequent at 56%; in Greece 63% of the initiatives deal with basic needs; while in Spain 63.2% are engaged in alternative economic activities. It is also interesting to analyse the values behind these initiatives. In this case, 2008 was an important watershed year. The initiatives set up before this date were driven by a desire to defend and demand human rights in order to achieve social justice.

Conversely, the main drivers of the initiatives that have emerged since 2008, are empowerment, participation, diversity and sustainability. National differences add to the framework of analysis: in Spain and Greece, the values of dignity are strongest, while in Italy, the values of emancipation in terms of social co-responsibility "*where people grow, make and do things for each other*" are more important (LIVEWHAT, 2016, p. 64).

Regarding the goals of these initiatives, the need to overcome the effects of the crisis and austerity measures prevails in Greece: "*Solidarity cannot be conceived outside the backdrop that austerity has carved, as it arises as an alternative horizon for people's lifeworlds, while dictating immediate action*" (Rakopoulos, 2016, p. 144). In Italy, the main purpose is to create alternative economic practices, and in Spain it is to bring about social change through collective action.

The initiatives come about as a reaction to the effects of the crisis but, as some studies confirm (Cruz et al., 2017; Guidi and Andretta, 2015; Putnam, 1995, 2004), they are concentrated in large urban areas. In other words, in areas where resources, social capital and a deep-rooted participatory tradition,[7] act as a "propulsive" force, feeding and supporting the presence of spaces where action and freedom can take place. According to Cristancho and Loukakis (2018), this dependence on social contexts that are rich in resources and opportunities could be a barrier, as it could reduce reliance on the substantive freedoms and inclusive development created through local collective actions.

[7]These results have also been confirmed in research conducted by Blanco and Cruz (2014), in Catalonia. In particular, focusing on Barcelona, the research shows that initiatives with an innovative social profile would not be found in rich or poor neighbourhoods, but rather in those with a strong tradition of social mobilization, which are culturally vibrant (for example, the "Gracia" neighbourhood).

2.2.1 Information Box: Collective Initiatives for Food Security in Italy, Spain and Greece

Barikamà is a social cooperative of migrants that was created thanks to the support of community buying groups, known in Italy by the acronym GAS (Gruppi di Acquisto Solidali), and other local initiatives in **Rome (Italy)**. Suleman, Aboubakar, Sialiki, Modibo, Ismael and Moussa are six young men from Mali. They crossed the desert on foot in one year. During that excruciating journey, many of their friends and travel companions did not survive. After that, they arrived in Libya and then they travelled by boat to finally land on the Italian coast.

At first, they moved to Rosarno (Calabria, southern Italy) where they started work in the orange harvest. Migrants work from 8 to 12 hours a day, with wages that range between 20 and 25 euros per day, in working environments with little or no safety measures at all. These debilitating labour conditions lead to human rights violations and basic capabilities deprivation, firstly in health: these people suffer from diseases related to the absence of safety measures, malnourishment and undernourishment. An insecure job determines housing conditions that are degrading from a socio-sanitary point of view, such as makeshift dwellings and overcrowding (De Filippo et al., 2012).

In January 2010, after taking part in a protest against exploitation and racism, the six migrants moved to Rome, where they came across people who belonged to the GAS Movement. From that encounter, "Barikamà" started to rise as a new entity. Barikamà means "resilience" in the Bambara language, the national language of Mali.

Barikamà seems to be an alternative to the labour exploitation of migrants in the agricultural sector, an alternative to illegality and criminality. In fact, they also run a business in Rome on confiscated Mafia property. Therefore, Barikamà is a chance to have decent work through sustainable and ethical agriculture. Indeed, it allows people with physical and mental disabilities to work in organic agriculture.

O Allos Anthropos (The Other Human), is an initiative designed to collectively address the growing food insecurity in **Athens (Greece)**. Cooking on the street together and eating together with no distinction made between those who are in need and those who are not. Every day, in the main squares of Athens, people gather and share meals together: tourists, students, homeless, migrants, etc. This is a way to prevent the social isolation of those who live in a state of poverty, while respecting their dignity. It is the brainchild of Konstantinos Polyxronopoulos.

In 2009, Kostantino lost his job at age 45 and was forced to return to live with his mother. The loss of his job and the difficulties in finding a new job led him to a period of deep emotional instability. The mobilization and the ferment generated by the protests of the Indignados in Syntagma Square in 2011, drove him to react and, above all, to follow up on the energy of the square. He views food as a "social factor" that can connect people, regardless of their political opinions. The idea for a social kitchen became concrete when Konstantino saw at a *laiki* (farmers' market) in Athens two children rummaging through the garbage and contending for the food they found.

The idea for "O Allos Anthropos" came from the concept of cooking collectively and socially.

Since then, Kostantino's project has extended, contagiously spreading the solidarity and, to date, there are 22 social kitchens in Greece, one in Turkey (Bodrum) and one in Spain (Barcelona).

In **Barcelona (Spain), Espigoladors** is an organization that collects fruit and vegetables from the field or supermarkets that cannot be sold for aesthetic reasons. The recovered produce is then distributed to charity groups, which in turn provide people in need with fresh fruit and vegetables.

Any produce that is not donated is transformed into jams, sauces and sold at 46 stores with the label "Es imperfect" ("It's imperfect"). By recovering and processing this produce, Espigoladors aims to promote social inclusion and foster a circular eco-sustainable and social economy.

It is an example of an initiative that links the problem of food insecurity to one of food waste, and is in line with the "Estratègia d'Impuls de la Política Alimentària 2016–2019" and the Charter for Food Sovereignty in Zaragoza in 2014. Both documents connect environmental sustainability projects to ones regarding inclusive development.

3 Collective Actions of Solidarity and Their Impact in Terms of Capabilities

3.1 Capabilities and the Social Dimension of Freedoms

This book takes as its theoretical framework the capability approach, which offers an interesting context for the study of people's real living conditions, in terms of substantive freedoms (Robeyns, 2000).

Starting from a critical analysis of utilitarianism (Bentham, 1823) and primary needs (Rawls, 1971), the capability approach outlines an alternative answer to the question "Equality of what?", which also became the title of a work by the economist Amartya Sen in 1979. Therefore, the capability approach is conceived as part of a broader reflection on egalitarian justice. This reflection shifts the focus from income, GDP and material goods to the real freedoms enjoyed by people in being able to choose between different ways of life (Sen, 2000).

In the 1990s, the capability approach of Amartya Sen,[1] together with the efforts of Mahbub ul Haq, chief founder of the Human Development Report, contributed to the emergence and consolidation of an alternative approach to development and the dominant economic paradigm in the 1980s, which was based on a strong correlation between economic growth and the expansion of individual human choices.

Indeed, the failure of the trickle-down economics principle was increasingly evident. According to this theory, wealth flows downward to reach all strata of society (by

[1]When Amartya Sen was awarded the Nobel Prize for Economics in 1998, the Wall Street Journal labelled him "the ambassador" of the confused ideas of the leftist establishment. In doing so, the Wall Street Journal failed to consider the influence played by Adam Smith in his thought and also Sen's own contribution to the emergence of a new idea of development to replace the conception that dominated the economic mainstream (Evans, 2002).

D. Bernaschi, *Collective Actions of Solidarity against Food Insecurity*, RaumFragen: Stadt – Region – Landschaft, https://doi.org/10.1007/978-3-658-31375-3_3

distributing the positive effects of economic growth), thus ending poverty. However, growing inequalities and social problems (i.e. crime, HIV, poverty) were also strongly present in countries with robust economic growth (Deneulin and Shahani, 2009; Deneulin and McGregor, 2009).

All these considerations and empirical evidence led to the adoption of a new perspective of analysis that looks at human development in terms of a growing process of substantive freedoms (Sen, 2000). According to this perspective, the main purpose of development is to create an environment that allows all people to live a healthy, long and creative life (Haq, 1996), to expand their capabilities (UNDP, 1990), and to realise their personal life projects.

The capability approach points out how economic growth can coexist with important social injustices. Economic growth, income and GDP[2] are the "means" and not the "end" of development. Focusing on them alone could, in fact, lead to a distorted analysis of the living conditions experienced by people. For this reason, it is crucial to focus on how these means are actually converted into well-being, paying attention to individual characteristics and social context. Indeed, individuals present differences in terms of age, gender, physical conditions and also live in different social and institutional conditions, therefore, their ability to convert income and goods[3] into achievements can vary significantly (Sen, 2003).

Capability arises as a comprehensive approach which simultaneously contains Adam Smith's (1759) reference to the living conditions necessary for enjoying essential freedoms, Marx's (1875) thought about freedoms and the richness of human diversity, and Aristotle's *eudaimonia*, that is self-realisation and the fulfilment of one's potential (Nussbaum, 1988).

Originally used for the analysis of inequalities in developing countries, in recent years, interest has also grown in its application in the North World's social contexts and, therefore, in economically developed societies, where it is crucial to overcome the weaknesses of the mainstream economic development analysis. Thus, "*the process of*

[2]GDP measures the level of wealth in a country; in other words, it measures the final goods and services produced in a given year in a specific country. Basically, GDP measures commodities multiplied by value. The diffusion and popularity of GDP as an indicator of well-being are due to its ability to be succinct and the fact that it is easy to understand. The limitations of this indicator were pointed out by its own founding father, the economist Kuznets. In 1933, Kuznets was commissioned by the US Department of Commerce to work on an indicator to monitor the country's economic performance after the 1929 crisis. From the beginning, Kuznets highlighted the discrepancy between a measure of production and people's real well-being. In fact, GDP does not take into account the quality of production, its environmental impact and growing social inequalities.

[3]Capability approach literature often refers to an example proposed by Robeyns (2005, p. 98–99), on the use of the "bicycle". The bicycle is an important means for achieving the capability of "being able to move freely" and, therefore, of "being independent". Nevertheless, if a person has some form of disability or lives in a context where there is no road access, ownership of the bicycle becomes irrelevant to his or her well-being.

economic development has to be concerned with what people can and cannot do, e.g. whether they can live long, escape avoidable morbidity, be well-nourished, be able to read, write and communicate, take part in literary and scientific pursuits, and so forth" (Sen, 1984, p. 497).

The capability approach simultaneously contains a study on the living conditions actually experienced by people and an analysis of the real freedoms that can be chosen from various combinations of "functionings". Functionings can cover the most basic conditions (being well-nourished, educated and escaping preventable diseases), to those of a more sophisticated nature, such as taking part in the life of the community and having self-respect (Salais, 2009; Sen, 2003).

The term "functionings" describes states of "being" and "doing". In other words, they are human achievements (Robeyns, 2005, p. 95); whereas "capabilities" represent the opportunities to achieve functionings, therefore being free or being able to "do" or "be" something (Von Jacobi et al., 2015; Sen, 1997, 1999, 2002, 2004).

Sen points out that, in order to be defined as decent or, to use his words, a "Good Life", a person's life must be the result of a free choice "*and not one in which the person is forced into a particular life— however rich it might be in other respects*" (Sen, 1985, p. 69–70).

From Sen's point of view, freedom has a double meaning. The first concerns the dimension of opportunity, that is, the dimension of capabilities and, therefore, the real opportunities a person has to choose from various functionings. The second concerns the process-related dimension of choosing and, therefore, the ability to act according to what is considered important. In the latter case, the reference relates to agency, which is the third keyword of the capability approach, after capabilities and functionings.

Agency relates to freedom defined as the "ability" to do and achieve any goals that people value and have reason to value. An agent is a person who acts and brings about change (Sen, 1999, p. 19). Lack of agency is seen in an oppressed and passive person who lacks the freedom to make decisions. Agency depends not only on personal characteristics, but also on the specific social and normative context (Narayan, 2005; Narayan et al., 2000; Ibrahim and Alkire, 2007; Alkire, 2002, 2005). In fact, for a person to act as an "agent", it is necessary that he or she enjoys the freedom to receive an education, the freedom of expression and association. Such freedoms allow him or her to develop, express and promote his or her ideas in a public context. Therefore, a person is free to "be" and to "do" something only in a context that fosters freedoms and where access to resources and rights is mediated by legal channels.

As Severine Deneulin (2008, p. 118) points out, agency is not a *tabula rasa*, but the result of particular social structures. In this regard, Deneulin offers an interesting example: a woman forced to accept an arranged marriage lacks the agency to reject it, because the social structures that shape the reality around her do not support her in this sense. This woman will only be able to gain agency to refuse the decisions of others, thanks to education and government programmes that promote and support gender issues, providing her the tools/means to challenge the pre-established order.

In other words, individual agency depends on the existence of social, normative and collective structures that can promote freedoms. Moreover, the exercise of agency influences the social context, contributing to the realisation of those basic conditions required for the enjoyment of actual freedoms (Alkire and Deneulin, 2009).

Indeed, the development of capabilities cannot take place without the participation of people in political and social affairs and, therefore, without the involvement of people in the decision-making process (Sen, 1999). This leads to the enhancement of participation and public debate as the expressions of the freedom of agency. If by development we mean the process of expanding substantive freedoms (Dreze and Sen, 2002), then we assume that there is no development without democracy. Actually, economic growth can occur even when democratic institutions have failed (Sen, 1999).

Agency, functionings, and capabilities are the cornerstone of an alternative approach to welfare and development; an approach that goes beyond the limits of previous economic and philosophical theories. In fact, the theoretical structure of the capability approach finds its genesis and strength in Sen's critical reflection of utilitarianism (Bifulco and Mozzana, 2011). Utilitarians evaluate well-being in terms of utilities achieved[4] and consider the individual a *homo oeconomicus* who acts only to maximise his personal interest.

With the capability approach, Sen aims to broaden the horizons of the analysis. His approach restores richness and complexity to the nature of human behaviour, by shifting the focus from utility to human capabilities, which are in turn embedded in a mutually interconnected relationship with the social dimension.

Capabilities are linked to a socio-institutional context, one that can either constrain or promote people's life chances (Beckert, 2010). For this reason, the concept of capabilities aims to highlight the presence of an empowering process that "combines" (Nussbaum, 1988; 2000; 2003) the individual dimension with the social, relational and institutional one, in a conversion of resources into effective opportunities (Sen, 1992a,b; Bonvin and Farvaque, 2007; Bonvin and Rosenstein, 2015; Bonvin and Thelen, 2003; Salais, 2003, 2009; Bonvin, 2012).

As Dahrendorf (1993, 1996, 2006, 2009) points out, people's "life chances" are affected by a combination of rights (entitlements) and material/immaterial goods (provisions), as well as by "ligatures", that is, components such as social and solidarity relations, the institutions and values that structure people's actions and identities socially.

"*Flourishing individuals generally need and depend on functional families, cooperative and high-trust societies, and social contexts which contribute to the development of individuals who choose 'valuable capabilities'*" (Stewart and Deneulin, 2002, p. 68).

In synthesis, what people can "do" and "be" and their freedom of agency, can be described by a dynamic flow (Figure 3.1). It starts from the endowments, that is, the

[4]In Bentham's traditional version, utility is analysed in terms of pleasure/happiness, whereas, according to later implementations, it is regarded as a numerical representation of choices made.

goods and resources owned at an individual/household level, and from the legal channels to legitimately access resources, then passes through the conversion factors linked to personal, social, environmental or contextual characteristics (Bonvin and Farvaque, 2007; Chiappero-Martinetti and Venkatapuram, 2014), and leads to capabilities and, hence, to real opportunities. At this point of the flow, agency steps in, transforming opportunities into functionings, that is, human achievements, which in turn affects endowments, replicating the flow in a "continuous" motion.

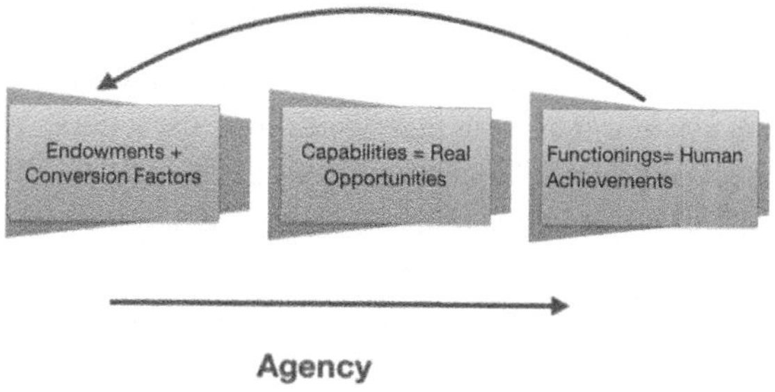

Figure 3.1 The capability approach's dynamic flow. *Source* Author's elaboration

3.2 The Social Perspective of Capabilities: A Critical Review

Despite the unquestionable contribution of Amartya Sen's thought to the study and analysis of social inequalities (Evans, 2002), the capability approach has been criticised for its individualistic nature and for the lack of attention it pays to the social and collective dimension. Indeed, some critics of this approach accuse the involving of *methodological individualism*[5] (Stewart and Deneulin, 2002) and charge Sen with being a "Manchester liberal" (Evans, 2002). According to them, the capability approach does not place the right emphasis on the contribution of the collective action (Stewart, 2005; Ibrahim, 2006, 2013, 2017).

Robeyns (2005), however, responds to this criticism by pointing out that the capability approach embraces individualism, but one that is ethical[6] in nature. Hence, the individual described by the capability approach is one who is immersed in the social context in which he or she lives, and whose opportunities are affected by social circumstances and public policy.

[5]By methodological individualism we mean the approach whereby all social phenomena can be explained and analysed, considering individuals and their characteristics: "*Any social phenomenon or social change can be explained in terms of the motivation and behavior of the individuals involved*" (Ballet et al. 2007, p. 186).

[6]According to Robeyns (2000; 2005, p. 107; 2008, p.90) "ethical individualism" means an analysis of social structures and institutions that takes account of the contribution they make to people's well-being. People are the focal space of any moral concern.

What is particularly important in ethical individualism is what happens to each individual within society. In contrast, if the focus of any concern were the group (i.e. family, community or social), this would lead to any inequalities within it being overlooked (Deneulin and Shahani, 2009). For example, in the case of women, this might be their subordinate station or the undernutrition of female children.[7]

Therefore, the capability approach's unit of interest is "the individual" recognised in its diversity (an explicit reference to Marx's thought[8]) and in its social dimension: "*Individual human beings with their various plural identities, multiple affiliations, and diverse associations are quintessentially social creatures with different types of social interactions, but their thoughts, choices, and actions are critically important parts of the society in which these individuals live*" (Sen, 2002, p. 81).

In answer to Stewart and Deneulin's criticism (2002), Sen underlines the importance of social context in influencing people, referring to the "adaptive preferences", or what Marx defines as the "false consciousness", of those people living in a state of chronic deprivation. More precisely, not finding the conditions to aspire to change, those who live in a state of social marginality (exploited workers, women in patriarchal societies, persecuted minorities and the poor), adapt their expectations to what is within their reach (Sen, 2003, 2009).

So, in the capability approach, the social and normative dimensions are embedded, but they are analysed only in light of their influence on individual well-being, and fail to focus on the effects related to the collective action: "*Societal arrangements, […] are investigated in terms of their contribution enhancing and guaranteeing the substantive freedoms of individuals*" (Sen, 1999, p. xiii). As also highlighted by Evans (2002) and Ibrahim (2006), when Amartya Sen, for example, praises the human development achievements of the Indian state of Kerala, he does not pay as much attention to the collective action underlying those successes. Therefore, he does not pay attention to the collective engine that has brought about the fruition of more rights and, consequently, has strengthened individual capabilities.

---

[7]Sen (1992c) highlighted the case of "missing women" in his studies, showing that, in some countries (China and India), there was a high rate of female infant mortality linked to social factors, such as selective abortion and a lack of attention to the health and nutrition of girls. This discrimination leads to an advantage for sons over daughters.

[8]Amartya Sen highlights the richness of human diversity, referring to Karl Marx's thought which, in "Critique of the Gotha Program" (1875), expresses a clear refusal for a class analysis and for an idea of equality oriented towards social levelling. "*Unequal individuals (and they would not be different individuals if they were not unequal) are measurable only by an equal standard in so far as they are brought under an equal point of view, are taken from one definite side only, for instance, in the present case, are regarded only as workers and nothing more is seen in them, everything else being ignored*" (Marx, 1875, p. 21–23).

Criticism of the capability approach focuses not only on the prevalence of an individualistic perspective of capabilities, but also on the lack of attention to the procedural, interactive and collective dimension of agency that leads to a "static" view of capabilities (Bifulco and Mozzana, 2011, p. 404). As pointed out by Zimmermann (2006), the concept of agency should be included within a broader analysis of social context affected by interaction between people. The theoretical structure of Sen's approach runs the risk of overlooking the importance of human interdependence and power relationships, in which the life chances of individuals are built (Dean, 2009).

In order to capture these dimensions, the capability approach should not only focus on the freedom of choice and the conversion of resources into actual achievements, but also on the process of generating and changing capabilities (Zimmermann, 2006); a process that results in a structured, interdependent relationship with the social context. The latter plays a crucial role in shaping the extent of both individual and collective freedom of choice, bringing out, to varying effect, a mechanism of path-dependency.

Moreover, it is necessary to highlight that the capability approach (in Sen's proposal) is an interesting opportunity which, with a view to subsequent integration work, can enhance the existing communication between the individual dimension of capabilities and the social and institutional context (De Munck, 2008). In this regard, recent literature and scholars are making efforts in order to develop and advance the original formulation of Sen's approach.

Indeed, some scholars have gone so far as to use the controversial concept of "collective capabilities" (Evans, 2002; Stewart, 2005; Ibrahim, 2006). Solava Ibrahim (2006, p. 404) defines them as *"the newly generated capabilities attained by virtue of their engagement in a collective action or their membership in a social network that helps them achieve the lives they value. They are not simply the sum (or average) of individual capabilities, but rather new capabilities that the individual alone would neither have nor be able to achieve, if he/she did not join a collectivity"*. In other words, the ability to choose a life that a person has reason to value, often depends on being able to act together with others. Thus, the individual's capabilities often depend on collective capabilities (Evans, 2002).

The empirical dimension of human relations, the role of collective agency and the role of public institutions (Bifulco and Mozzana, 2011) allow us to move from a static and individualistic perspective of capabilities to one that is interdependent, collective, dynamic and procedural (Figure 3.2). That is to say, it is important to emphasise the social dimension of ligatures and their contribution to the definition of life chances and individual capabilities.

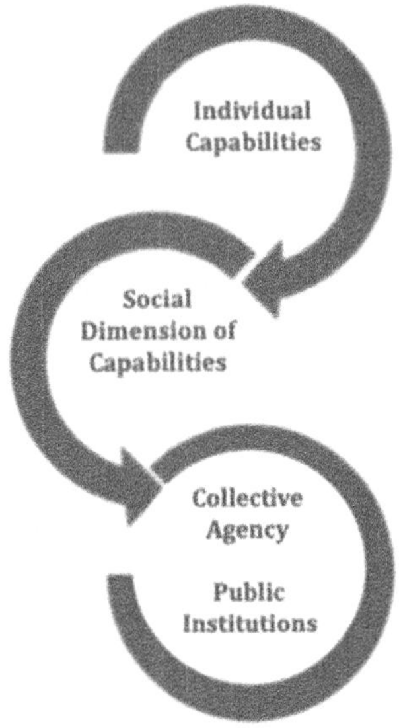

Figure 3.2 From the individual to the social dimension of capabilities. *Source* Author's elaboration

3.3 The Creative Power of Collective Agency

The genesis and evolution of individual capabilities are interdependent with the social and institutional context. From this perspective, change takes the shape of a social construction in which collective agency plays a key role.

The practice of collective agency cannot be coercively imposed and does not depend—at least, not mechanically—on the freedoms and rights that people enjoy and might lead them, almost automatically, to act collectively (Ballet et al., 2007). Instead, it is deeply embedded in public debate and the social interactions that contribute to the emergence of shared values and a sense of responsibility (Pelenc et al., 2015).

The exercise of collective agency is instrumental to the change, orienting policies towards a more careful promotion of capabilities (Fukuda-Parr, 2003). According to Ibrahim (2017), because of the constraints on individual agency—particularly in deprived communities—the role of collective agency is essential for the promotion of freedoms, choices and capabilities.

At this point, we should consider, for example, the concept of empowerment, which defines the process of expansion and strengthening of a person's agency. Of course, central to em-*power*-ment is the word "power", which does not refer to the common meaning of power "over things" or "over people", but to a power that binds the individual and the social dimension. In fact, it is the power to act, to create new opportunities and to make changes not only in one's own life but also in the context in which one operates. At the same time, it is also the power that derives from one's interdependence with others. It is the force that arises from collective action.

There is no official definition of "collective action" (Raushmayer et al., 2015), but we can outline its constitutive elements: a group of people who, through cooperative action on a voluntary basis, pursue shared goals and interests that go beyond the interest of the individual participant. Interaction between people (including when its structured into organised forms) through the exercise of collective agency can affect capabilities and achieve results that would be inaccessible at the individual level (Ibidem, 2015), owing to the lack of a system of rights/resources and legal channels to access them.

Collective action strengthens the capability for voice, that is, the capability to discuss, challenge and participate in a critical and active way (Hirschman, 2002). It also strengthens the ability to aspire to and imagine change (Appadurai, 2014), especially by those who live in conditions of deprivation and who, for this reason, lack resources and rights: "*To provide the poor with tools, and the voice, to navigate their way out of poverty*" (Rao and Walton, 2004, p. 361).

Using as an example the work of The Alliance[9] in Mumbai and its commitment to the rights of slum dwellers, Appadurai (2014) underlines how crucial it is to strengthen the ability of the poor to aspire (Thorp et al., 2003), on which depends the ability to conquer and exercise "protest" (Hirschman, 2002) to achieve effective change in the distribution of resources and access to them. What emerges, therefore, is that the ability to aspire and the capability for voice act together and mutually reinforce each other (Bifulco and Mozzana, 2011) on both an individual and a collective level.

Like Appadurai (2014), Krishna et al. (1997, p. 298) also highlight the role of collective action in fostering change: "*People with few resources other than their labor, intelligence, creativity and social networks, would be able through increasing self-reliance to achieve improvements in their lives across a range of sectors and areas*".

Therefore, the individual and collective dimensions reinforce each other. Indeed, strengthening a person's agency allows her to come out of social isolation and speak out in her own voice, a voice that is amplified by the collaboration of different social actors. In fact, collective actions can generate a change in power relations and, through a synergy with public institutions, contribute to creating conditions that enable substantive freedoms.

The creative power of collective action is affected by the existence of democratic institutions (the rights of associations, access to information and material resources) that can support the "acts of citizenship", about which Isin[10] (2009) writes. More precisely,

---

[9]The Alliance was established in 1987 from three different collective actions of solidarity in Mumbai (India): Society for the Protection of Area Resource Centers (NGO), National Slum Dwellers Federation (community-based organization) and Mahila Milan (organization of women living in poverty).

[10]The concept of "social acts" by Reinach (1983) is adopted by Isin (2009). Social acts precede the action and the actors, and are characterized by the fact that they break with routine, discipline and established practices, and also their power for reaction and transformation. "*We must focus on rupture rather than order but a rupture that enables the actor (that the act creates) to create a scene rather than follow a script*" (Isin, 2009, p.379).

those acts can transform strategies, orientations and technologies and encourage the transition from the status of "citizen, foreigner, outsider", to the status of "activist citizen" demanding his or her rights.

Following Mannheim (1968), dealing with social disintegration, democratic planning or planning for freedom through the direct involvement of social actors are all crucial for facing new and increasing structured social needs. Broader participation emerges as a real tool for empowerment (Schwan, 2017).

What people are free to do and be is not rigidly anchored in the individual dimension alone, but is the result of a complex and dynamic mechanism. This mechanism concerns the influence exerted by the social and normative context, which is affected by active participation and collective action (Salamon, 1994).

It is necessary to stress, however, that not all forms of collective actions lead to the broadening of human capabilities. Some groups, for example, despite claims of being on the side of people experiencing poverty, are in fact responsible for stoking social conflict (Stewart, 2005) and operate on the basis of cronyism (Ibrahim, 2012). Thus, some studies show a certain scepticism towards the role played by collective action (Cleaver, 1999; Das Gupta et al., 2000).

At the same time, other academic contributions convey a more optimistic perspective (Ostrom, 1990; Rakopoulos, 2014; D'Alisa et al., 2015; Kousis, 2017; Sotiropoulos, 2014; Bosi and Zamponi, 2015; Ibrahim, 2017; Simiti, 2017; Rauschmayer et al., 2015; Papadaki and Kalogeraki, 2018). Without underestimating the potential negative consequences of collective action, it is also essential that the collective dimension should not be excluded from the study on human capabilities. It is crucial to investigate its characteristics, the ways it operates and its normative approach, paying particular attention to its contribution in terms of substantive freedoms (Ibrahim, 2017).

3.4 Collective Actions of Solidarity in Terms of Social Co-responsibility: Individual Agency and Capability for Voice

This book adopts the concept of collective actions of solidarity which enables an in-depth look at the nature of the "creative chaos" referred to Dahrendorf (1989;1996; 2006; 2008), and specifically, all those social actors such as neighbourhood organisations, voluntary groups, self-subsistence networks, informal solidarity networks, civic networks, cooperatives and NGOs (Ibrahim and Hulme, 2010).

In the last decade and, hence, since the 2008 crisis, alongside studies on the effects of the economic crisis and the consequent policies to tackle it, extensive literature has emerged on those initiatives that are deeply rooted in the local dimension. Initiatives that deal with poverty and social exclusion, through a "*reaction/survival*" approach (e.g. food banks, social canteens) or by developing a "*new and more sustainable social system*" (e.g. community buying groups, urban gardens and alternative currencies).

The literature adopts different terminologies and lines of analysis to refer these initiatives: from the concept of collective action (Rauschmayer et al., 2015) to self-help groups (Ibrahim, 2006), to grassroots initiatives or community-based organisations (Dongier et al., 2018; Seyfang and Haxeltine, 2012). In some studies, the focus is on their resilient nature (Kousis, 2017; Arampatzi, 2017) and their politicisation (Bosi and Zamponi, 2015), and therefore their capacity to open public spaces for alternative political reflection. In others, they focus on their contribution in terms of social innovation (Blanco et al. 2014; Von Jacobi et al., 2015), or on the conditions that allow them to operate (Fioramonti and Kononykhina, 2014).

In this book, the analysis focuses on collective actions of solidarity as an expression of a collective agency, that can act as a driving force for capabilities. The basis of these initiatives is not only the drive of citizens for greater involvement and participation. Indeed, it is possible to discern an idea of social solidarity that is unifying and universal (Beck, 2003) the expression of "co-responsibility" towards society, and not purely as *volunteering* for others (Crespi, 2013). Given the "constitutive sociality" of human beings, social solidarity emerges as emancipation through participation in collective life (Ibid., 2013).

The concept of social solidarity is therefore presented in its twofold guise (Elias, 1988): as a lubricant of social relations through a mechanism of social "bridging" between people (Putnam, 2000), on the one hand, and as an expression of autonomy, emancipation and agency, on the other.

In fact, the forms of expression that social solidarity can take, highlight the active role that social actors play in discerning the change taking place (Leonardi, 2001, 2009, 2018), and the opportunities that the crisis can offer. That is, if by crisis we mean a period of "creative destruction" (Eder, 2015; Leonardi, 2018). In this, social solidarity presents itself as an expression of a creative and transformative power; in other words, as a process of "world-making" (Calhoun, 1998, 2002) that is forward-looking (Crow, 2002; Papadaki and Kalogeraki, 2018). It emerges, therefore, not only as a means to react to the consequences of the crisis, but also as a strategic tool for boosting collective empowerment and social transformation.[11]

Referring to collective actions of solidarity arising as a reaction to the effects of the crisis in Greece, Rakopoulos (2016, p. 142) defines solidarity as "*An idea inspiring people in contexts of everyday life in crisis. In an array of activities that includes social clinics, social pharmacies, anti-middleman food markets and soup kitchens, the grassroots solidarity economy of a country threatened by rapid pauperisation has borne a vivid reality that emerged during (and perhaps partly because of) the 'crisis'* ".

Environmental challenges, poverty and food insecurity are complex and multidimensional issues that require the wider participation of all social actors, through which to

[11]For further details see: Bernaschi, D., Leonardi, L. 2020. "The binomial food and cities: the local dimension of food security from the perspective of global sociology.", In *Rassegna Italiana di Sociologia,* Il Mulino -forthcoming publication-.

define shared action strategies (in this regard, some argue the emergency and the transformative potential of reflexive governance[12]). Thus, these are problems that demand a greater sense of responsibility towards society, for greater "care of the world" (Pulcini, 2009). The result is the conceptualisation of solidarity as an essential condition for ensuring the survival of humankind (Crespi, 2013; Crespi and Moscovoci, 2001) and enabling inclusive development.

Consequently, the responsibility goes beyond the individual dimension and, instead, emphasises the social nature of people: "*The good of others is not just a constraint on this person's pursuit of her own good; it is a part of her good*" (Nussbaum, 2006, p. 158). Responsibility, even before it is the fulfilment of an ethical duty, is a right that derives from the exercise of freedom: "*I turn from rights to correlative duties [...] Since freedoms are important, people have reason to ask what they should do to help each other in defending or promoting a retrospective freedoms*" (Sen, 2004, p. 338).

As Sen points out in the essay "Individual freedom as a social commitment" (1997, p. 56-57), the concept of individual freedom includes, on the one hand, everything that enables us to live as responsible and active individuals (e.g. health care, public education, freedom from poverty and hunger). On the other hand, it also includes the freedom to participate in political and social decision-making processes. A freedom that also assumes the rank of social commitment.

This reciprocity also finds expression in the definition of agency by Alkire and Deneulin (2009, p. 45, resuming Sen, 1985), in which the freedom of agency refers not only to effective power and direct control over actions at the individual level, but also to the responsibility of operating as a member of a community. It also refers to the exercise of freedom which does not involve coercive power relations, but which leads to the achievement of both personal and collective goals.

Hence, this conceptualisation leads to an exercise of agency that is not limited to purely individual interests, but also includes social co-responsibility. It is in this regard, that Sen makes his criticism of *homo oeconomicus*: the individual is not a rational fool (Sen, 1977) focused only on the maximisation of personal interests, but has multiple aims that even encompass the solidarity with others.

---

[12]Reflexive governance opens new social and political spaces, involving public, private and civic sectors, which allow a shared reflection on the practices to be adopted for the transition to sustainability (Marsden, 2013). Consider, for example, the experience of Food Policy Councils which involve public institutions, NGOs, neighbourhood networks, civic networks, associations to discuss and approve policies concerning the food system. Studies on reflexive governance refer to the paradigm of "reflexive modernity" developed by Giddens (1990), Beck (1992) and Lash (1993): "*Reflexivity is the capacity of individual subjects to direct their awareness toward themselves, reflecting upon their own practices, and constantly examining and reforming these practices in the light of incoming information*" (Giddens, 1990, p. 38).

Therefore, the interpersonal dimension is part of the framework of capabilities. As the members of a society benefit from each other's interaction, they must also accept mutual obligations (Sen, 2004). In this way, the idea of freedom is found in a dual relationship: on the one hand, with individual choice and, on the other, with collective social responsibility.

In terms of social co-responsibility, collective actions of solidarity take the form of a two-faced Janus (Figure 3.3., p. 28). On the one hand, they strengthen the agency and the individual capabilities of those who benefit directly or indirectly from the resources and/or rights made available to them. On the other hand, they act as an expression of a sense of shared responsibility, through networks of cooperation with other initiatives and public institutions. They work towards an effective fight against the structural conditions of poverty, enhancing the voice of those who live in conditions of deprivation and social marginality. Giving voice, therefore, to those who do not have one, owing to a lack of resources/rights, means that these collective actions of solidarity can contribute to social change.

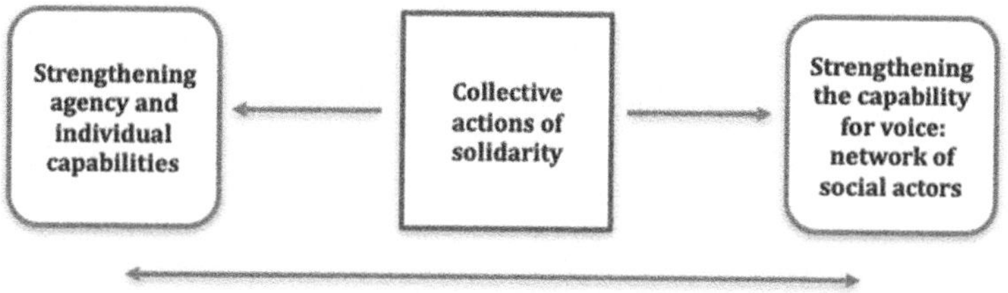

Figure 3.3 The impact of collective actions of solidarity in terms of agency and capability for voice. *Source* Author's elaboration

Individual agency and the network of social actors are mutually strengthened. The expansion of the agency of the beneficiaries enables them to acquire substantive freedom and the ability to foster change. As highlighted by Appadurai (2014), the ability to imagine change, while relying on individual emancipatory actions from the present, builds bridges to a more desirable future. The ability to aspire appears as the "meta-capacity" that allows the ability to react to unfold for others.

Empowerment consists precisely in the process of strengthening the freedoms to act and to plan. Thanks to the support of collective actions of solidarity, beneficiaries can gain the power to aspire to change, using the facilities and resources made available by collective initiatives. Moreover, by strengthening the capability for voice through a network of cooperation between different social actors, collective action determines changes in social structures, in turn influencing the expansion process of individual agency.

The Empirical Research

4

4.1 Case Studies and Methods

This book presents the results of an empirical research project on food insecurity in Italy, Spain and Greece. The reason these countries were chosen is not only because they are often associated with a "Southern European" welfare model in literature, but mainly because, according to the latest Eurostat data (2019), they show an increase in the percentage of people who are at risk of poverty and social exclusion. Despite this, the countries show many differences between them. By moving away from a rigid conception of modellisation, the paths required to tackle food insecurity will be many and varied even at local level.

The research departs from a merely descriptive purpose of social phenomena to embrace, instead, an analysis aimed at:

- identifying the main drivers of food insecurity;
- assessing the impact of local initiatives in terms of capabilities; and
- highlighting a different problematisation of food insecurity, linking it to the issue of food waste and, therefore, to the inefficiencies of the production system, or to a dimension that is more linked to people's substantive freedoms.

For this purpose, secondary data were used (e.g. main contributions from academic literature and documents related to grey literature—reports of international organisations, articles, reports on the activities of NGOs, national and EU public documents), as well as primary data collected through interviews with key informants, participant observation and in-depth semi-structured interviews, both with the beneficiaries and the coordinators of the collective actions of solidarity. In total, 110 qualitative interviews were conducted in Rome, Barcelona and Athens, from November 2016 to June 2019.

D. Bernaschi, *Collective Actions of Solidarity against Food Insecurity*, RaumFragen: Stadt – Region – Landschaft, https://doi.org/10.1007/978-3-658-31375-3_4

The first stage of the empirical research in Rome, Barcelona and Athens started with an investigation of the socio-economic characteristics of the three different contexts. Through the snowballing selection method, we proceeded to interview people from academia and from the political and the third sectors. This preliminary study made it possible to identify the three initiatives on which to focus the research. In Rome, the decision was made to select the Emporium of Solidarity of Caritas, in Barcelona, the Solidarity Card and, in Athens, the Solidarity Kitchen of the NGO Kipoda.

The Emporium in Rome is an initiative promoted by Caritas. It is a rescued food supermarket where people can shop free of charge using a card. People can freely choose what to purchase. The products come from company donations or from the European FEAD programme for indigent people.

Solidarity Card is a shared blueprint but independently managed by Caritas and the Municipality of Barcelona. Basically, it is a card which can be used at any supermarket or neighbourhood shop, which allows people to get on with their daily lives.

The Solidarity Kitchen in Athens is a soup kitchen where meals donated by restaurants or military cafeterias are distributed. The beneficiaries are given an appointment to collect meals for their family. The appointment allows people to avoid long queues, which safeguards their dignity.

These initiatives were chosen because of their formalised or institutionalised format. They highlight the social nature of capabilities and the impact of collective action in defining individual life chances. Once the initiatives were identified, they were then analysed in depth, in order to know their background, normative nature and influence in terms of their beneficiaries' capabilities. With this in mind, semi-structured in-depth interviews were conducted with both the coordinators and the beneficiaries of the initiatives. A total of 66 interviews were carried out. Two different interview tracks were created, one for the coordinators and the other for the beneficiaries.

As the capability approach suggests, it is necessary for the people involved in the development process, to play an active role as agents and not as passive recipients of external aid. For this reason, this research considered it crucial to give a direct voice to the people involved, whether they were acting as coordinators or beneficiaries of the initiatives. In this way, knowledge of a given social phenomenon comes from the bottom, rather than from some pre-established theory.

4.1.1 Emporium of Solidarity, Solidarity Card and Solidarity Kitchen: The Perspective of the Coordinators

The interviews with the coordinators were structured in such a way as to bring to the fore the organisational and social characteristics of the initiatives and the normative approach underlying the measures adopted.

The analysis of the interviews is divided into five main parts. The first part is intended to investigate the origin of the initiative: in what social context it is working, why it was created and with what purposes. The second part aims to look more closely at the characteristics of the action: what it consists of, how it is structured and to whom it is addressed. The third part goes even deeper to highlight how the initiative works in detail, by answering the following questions:

- Are the criteria for selecting beneficiaries universal or constrained?
- Is the normative approach focusing on releasing the beneficiaries from need, or is it capability-oriented?
- Are mono- or multi-dimensional measures put into action? In other words, do the measures merely compensate for shortcomings or do they activate the beneficiaries themselves?

The fourth part of the interview focuses on analysing the methods used for collecting and distributing food resources. The aim was to determine whether:

- the organisational structure of the initiative uses food waste products and/or surplus products from the market production system;
- the initiatives use an approach designed to activate the beneficiaries or merely encourages the passive receipt of goods that are selected by others; and
- there is an awareness of the different nutritional, cultural and relational needs of people.

The last part is structured to highlight the existence or the lack of any relationships with the other social actors. Hence, the networks with other collective actions of solidarity and the relationships with the local public institutions is analysed. The idea is to determine the nature of these relationships: whether they are characterised by a collaborative approach or whether, instead, public institutions are delegating the resolution of social issues to collective action.

Furthermore, in the case of a cooperative relationship, the aim is to understand how it can affect the food insecurity issue. Do these relationships target the causes of food insecurity with a long-term strategy or do they only provide emergency short-term measures designed merely to bridge the gap?

4.1.2 Operationalising the Capability Approach: Life Trajectories of the Beneficiaries

The interviews with the beneficiaries were carried out through a process of operationalisation of the capability approach. The operationalisation of the capability approach, that is, the concrete application of the concepts of agency, functionings and capabilities "*the diverse sequence of transforming a theory into an object of practical value*" (Comin,

2001, p. 1), is somewhat complicated, leading some researchers (Srinivasan, 1994) in the early 1990 s to seriously doubt its effective use for empirical purposes.

"*The multidimensional-context-dependent-counterfactual-normative nature of the capability approach might prevent it from having practical and operational significance*" (Comim, 2008, p. 159).

Different views and perspectives of analysis emerge in the capability literature. While some focus on the challenge of converting a concept into something that can be implemented in empirical analysis (Atkinson and Bourguignon, 2000), others focus on the contribution that sociological analysis can offer to the comprehensive methodology of capabilities (Zimmermann, 2006), and others yet elaborate useful criteria for the practical use of capability. Robeyns (2003) points this out with these three specific steps:

1. Identifying a list of relevant capabilities;
2. Deciding whether the analysis focuses on capabilities and, therefore, on opportunities or, otherwise, on functionings;
3. Defining a system of weights to assign to the different capabilities or functionings.

Hence, any empirical study that aims to use the capability approach must determine which capabilities to consider (Von Jacobi et al., 2015). This selection does not contradict Sen's position on the importance of democratic dynamics (participation, public debate, voice), from the normative point of view of the policies. The selection, in the research framework, is driven by an analytical intent.[1]

There are different methodologies for selecting capabilities; some are based on a *top-down* approach, others on a *bottom-up* approach and, therefore, on participatory research methods (e.g. focus groups). This book utilises three main *top-down* sources: the research goals; the Millennium Development Goals; and the "*Missing Dimensions of poverty*" developed by the *Oxford Human Development Initiative*.

Regarding the selection of the questions, as Salais evidenced (2009), there are different strategies for collecting information about a person's capabilities. From such surveys (e.g. the Eurobarometer), which measure the level of satisfaction and are based on subjective perception, to others which establish beforehand that are functionings as the basis on which to assess people's living conditions. There are also methodologies that use questions which generate replies that are free from a subjective perception, such as: "Is maternity leave guaranteed in your work?"

This book is based on the latter approach and includes questions that highlight, on the one hand, material and immaterial functionings (e.g. health, nutrition, housing, work,

[1]In his studies on the high female mortality rate in certain societies and on the case of "missing women" (1992c), Sen himself makes certain choices, in relation to the spaces of analysis to be considered, in line with the objectives of the research and without ever attempting to be prescriptive.

education and social relations) and, on the other hand, the freedom to choose, act and realise one's life plans. The life plans that people "have reason to value" (Sen, 1999). The emphasis on "*have*" *reason to value* should be stressed, because it allows us to take into account all those constraints and opportunities that come from the social and institutional context in which a person lives and that guide, shape and hinder the achievement of what he or she values.

The objective of the interviews with the beneficiaries is to determine, through the reconstruction of their experiences, the interdependence of the individual and social dimension of capabilities. The interviews are, therefore, structurally designed to highlight a set of capabilities.

Seven main individual capabilities were identified:

1. health: physical and psychological health conditions;
2. education and training: the nature of one's education path and the freedom to choose it;
3. family well-being: housing and the role of the family in terms of help and influence;
4. social relations: the role of friends, participation in structured initiatives, exercise of the right to vote;
5. changes and life planning: most important decision taken in life, ability to create new opportunities, responsibility related to the implementation of their life plans;
6. economic security: nature of employment, social transfers and benefits;
7. food security: access to a food basket that meets their nutritional, cultural and social needs.

The focus of the interviews with the beneficiaries is not on what people "do" or "are". Through a longitudinal analysis (supported by the Nvivo software) and the reconstruction of their life paths, the research aims, on the contrary, to understand what people are "free to do and to be", and how the collective actions of solidarity affect their substantive freedoms.

People have different needs and life goals and, therefore, the nutritional, cultural and relational uses that they make of the resources made available to them, through the initiatives, differ considerably. The aim will be to reconstruct people's life trajectories, in order to bring out the enabling and disabling factors they have in common in terms of capabilities, and also, the influence played by the institutional context (for example, the absence of public measures on income support) and social context (job segregation for migrants, for example), on their ability to convert resources into effective freedoms.

The analysis of how collective actions of solidarity affect the beneficiaries' lives, is followed by an analysis of the different pathways of empowerment that are promoted. In other words, it highlights the extent to which they are capabilities-oriented or whether the approach is merely to "compensate for shortcomings".

4.1.3 *Capabilities-Oriented* Initiatives or "Compensation for Shortcomings" Initiatives

The initiatives investigated will be defined as *capabilities-oriented* or merely compensating for shortcomings, based on three main dimensions.

The first concerns the procedures for accessing the initiative; in other words, it is aimed at analysing whether the beneficiary's access to the initiative is universal or constrained by compliance with specific parameters. This point can be understood by reflecting on the distinction proposed by Sen (2000) between "human capital", with its economic return, and capabilities, in terms of substantive freedoms. Investing in human capital entails the risk of investing in those who can guarantee an economic return, with the risk of exclusion and the Matthew effect.[2] The capability approach, on the other hand, considers it crucial to invest in all people in terms of substantive freedoms, even in those who are socially excluded (Appadurai, 2014), and in this, the universality of access and rights plays a key role.

The second dimension concerns the normative approach underlying the actions proposed by the initiative. The intention is to understand whether the structure of the intervention aimed at tackling poverty and food insecurity, is designed to satisfy basic needs (e.g. distribution of clothes, food and medicines) or to strengthen the agency and the individual capabilities of those who benefit -directly or indirectly- from the resources and/or rights made available to them. Therefore, in the latter case, we are referring to a system of support and resources that aims to promote empowerment and a way out of social exclusion.

The third and final dimension regards the impact of the initiatives. Collective actions of solidarity are analyzed in terms of social co-responsibility (as we saw in Chapter 3). For this reason, the impact of initiatives should be addressed, firstly, by looking at their contribution in terms of social change. Expressing a sense of shared responsibility, through cooperation with other initiatives and public institutions, collective initiatives work towards strengthening the capability for giving voice. For this purpose, the nature of these collaborations will be analysed as follows: whether they are aimed at the promotion of capabilities and, therefore, the principle of social change, or are only aimed at compensating for shortcomings.

Secondly, the impact of the initiatives will be investigated by looking at their contribution to strengthening the agency of their beneficiaries. Specific emphasis will be placed on whether food resources are accessed through the active participation of beneficiaries or are merely passively received by them.

---

[2]In relation to redistributive policies, it refers to a process whereby newly available resources are distributed among people in proportion to what they already have.

Capabilities-oriented initiatives (see Figure 4.1, p. 34) are characterised by the following aspects:

a) universal access: investing in all people in need, not only in those who have a good chance of emerging from poverty and, to a certain extent, guaranteeing the success of the investment;
b) a normative approach to expanding the agency of beneficiaries through support that goes beyond food distribution, facilitating empowerment and strengthening individual capabilities;
c) the mobilisation of a network of collaboration between collective actions of solidarity and local public institutions through which to contribute, by strengthening the capability for voice, to create suitable environmental and social conditions for promoting individual capabilities;
d) the adoption of procedures enabling individual and active access to food resources, strengthening the agency of beneficiaries. In other words, people are free to make decisions about their own nutrition. Supporting the individual's choice, the conversion of resources into relevant functionings is encouraged.

	Type of access to the initiative	Normative Approach	Social solidarity impact	
			Capability for voice	Strengthening the agency of beneficiaries
			Type of collaboration between collective actions of solidarity and local public institutions	Type of access to food aid
Capabilities-oriented initiative	Universal	Expanding the agency and strengthening the capabilities of beneficiaries	Fostering capabilities	Active
Compensation for shortcomings initiative	Universal or Restricted	Satisfying basic needs	Compensation for shortcomings	Passive

Figure. 4.1 Type of food insecurity initiatives. *Source* Author's elaboration

In contrast, there are initiatives to "compensate for shortcomings", where access may either be universal or be restricted to those possessing certain criteria. In these initiatives, both the normative approach and the network of collaboration between collective actions of solidarity and public institutions are exclusively directed at meeting basic needs. Primary needs are accessed through a mechanism of passive receipt of the service, with no focus on the different nutritional, social and relational objectives and needs. The beneficiaries are, therefore, the recipients of foods that are standardised and/or recycled from the food waste reduction process, in other words, food chosen and prepared by other people.

The investigation on local food security initiatives allows two main research goals. Firstly, it reveals the influence the social and institutional dimension have on the generative process of one's capabilities. Secondly, it involves a dual analysis of collective actions: one concerns their contribution to the expansion of the agency and capabilities of the beneficiaries; and the other one regards the development, through a network of cooperation between collective actions of solidarity and local public institutions, of a fertile social ground for the promotion of capabilities.

Emporium of Solidarity, Solidarity Card and Solidarity Kitchen: The Impact of Social Solidarity in Terms of Capability for Voice

5

5.1 Rome: The Emporium of Solidarity

In Rome, the Caritas[1] Emporium of Solidarity is embedded in a context where socio-economic inequalities have strong "territorial" (Tomassi et al., 2016) and "social" connotations, where unskilled workers and the middle class face social exclusion and a rising cost of living (De Muro et al., 2011). Social difficulties[2] exist alongside the weaknesses of the institutional context (overwhelmed by the case of Mafia Capitale[3]) which

[1]The Italian Caritas is the pastoral body of the CEI, that is, the Italian Episcopal Conference (the Permanent Union of Catholic Bishops in Italy) which is responsible for charity works.

[2]Distance from the city centre is representative of distance in social terms and from opportunities. In Rome, there is a co-existence of at least "two cities": one that can benefit from the opportunities deriving from the economy of knowledge, while the other, is excluded from this development, where education levels and healthcare indicators are more similar to those of the southernmost parts of Italy than to those expected in the capital city (Tomassi et al., 2016, p. 13). What emerges is not only a gap between the centre and the suburbs, but also the existence of other problematic areas, such as, the eastern districts and the town of Ostia on the Roman coast.

[3]A mafia-type organization founded in Rome and whose identity was revealed in 2014. The charges against Mafia Capitale were that it had manipulated the allocation of public procurements, thanks to relationships between organized crime and certain public officials and politicians. The effects of Mafia Capitale overwhelmed the third sector. Indeed, several public tenders were suspended, and for this reason some cooperatives were forced to close and others to lay off workers.

D. Bernaschi, *Collective Actions of Solidarity against Food Insecurity*, RaumFragen: Stadt – Region – Landschaft, https://doi.org/10.1007/978-3-658-31375-3_5

essentially take the form of delegating the monitoring[4] and the resolution[5] of social problems to collective actions of solidarity.

The Emporium was founded in Rome in 2008.[6] Until then, the main focus of Caritas Rome was extreme poverty (migrants, homeless people and psychiatric patients); however, the effects of the crisis required a change in its assistance programmes. In fact, the growing number of people who, owing to the loss of their jobs or insufficient wages, were unable to provide for their own food, led Caritas to think up a different initiative to help them. Indeed, families experiencing serious deprivation -for the first time- would never have queued up at traditional charity soup kitchens for several reasons, including, for example, a deep sense of shame.

The Emporium aims to overcome the social stigma linked to soup kitchens and food parcels. For this reason, it is structured like a real supermarket, to reconstruct an environment of normal everyday life, where people are activated to come, do their shopping and choose what to buy. The first Emporium to open in Rome was the "Cittadella della Carità" (City of Charity), in district VII, and resembles a medium-sized supermarket.

The City of Charity is equipped with a modern structure that gives a welcoming feeling to visitors, providing them with a green area and places where they can socialise. At the centre, there is a small church and all the Caritas facilities are located around it, including: offices, free dental clinics, a care home and the Emporium building.

In Rome, there are two other Caritas Emporiums, one completed in 2011 in "Spinaceto", district IX, and one which opened in 2015 in "Trionfale", district XIV. Both are small neighbourhood shops that are a way to increase the sense of belonging to the community: "*They represent the idea that a community takes charge of the fragile in its area*" (Caritas Secretary in Rome).

At the Emporium, a score card is used to obtain groceries. There are two cards: the family card and the children's card (for minors under 2 years). The cards have a certain number of points depending on the number and type of household.

Adhering to a circular form of economy, the Emporium connects the problem of food insecurity to the surpluses of the market production system. The Emporium's products

---

[4]All investigations into socio-economic conditions in Rome were carried out by Caritas and the Community of St.Egidio (a lay movement with a Catholic influence). Although they provide crucial information, there are limitations related to their individual databases.

[5]The Lazio Region's tender "Un taglio alla povertà" provides financial support to collective anti-poverty initiatives.

[6]The first two Emporiums were established by Caritas in Rome in 2008, and were followed shortly afterwards by branches in Prato (Tuscany). So far, the number of Emporiums in Italy has grown significantly. There are 60 (CSVNet, 2015) Caritas Emporiums, not including, therefore, those set up by trade unions or other associations.

are donated through the European FEAD programme[7] (Fund for European Aid to the Most Deprived), the large-scale distribution system[8] and private food donors. Food donations from businesses are incentivised by a special legislative framework with tax benefits (Good Samaritan Law of 2003, and Law No. 166 of 19 August 2016).

Despite the fact that FEAD products no longer contain a label identifying them as "*Products for the Most Deprived*", beneficiaries continue to prefer branded products.

"*When they get European products, it is as if people say to themselves: 'I'm poor, I need charity'. They know they need help, but sometimes it would be better not to see it spelled out so blatantly*" (Emporium Volunteer).

The Emporium is one of the supports offered alongside others such as assistance in finding a job, Italian language classes for foreigners, free medical care, support in paying domestic bills, an anti-usury service and the Family Fund.[9]

Access to the Emporium is only given to people who are experiencing a temporary period of difficulty, which facilitates projects to bring them out of poverty. For situations of chronic poverty or in the case of elderly people, the preference -in many cases- is to continue with food parcels. A mechanism for selecting beneficiaries leads to investing in people, who can ensure a return on the social investment, and excludes situations of severe deprivation.

From the empirical analysis, the Emporium is an expression of "social solidarity" in the form of collective action, an action that aims to strengthen the capability for voice of those who are forced into a situation of deprivation. In this sense, the Emporium succeeds in having an impact on the community through two different types of intervention. The first creates a strong network of collaboration with other collective initiatives (for example, the Community of Capodarco[10]), and introduces projects for the social integration of people with different types of social fragility (former prisoners, disabled people). This contributes to a sense of active citizenship with a significant impact in terms of social inclusion.

The second involves actions of advocacy in "national" public institutions in order to develop effective anti-poverty policies. Caritas is one of the thirty-five organisations that make up the "Alliance against Poverty" founded in 2013, which has made a decisive

[7]Most of these European products are long-term food items with special packaging that carries the FEAD aid label, with the specification that they cannot be sold.

[8]The majority of the donations are near their expiry date, or may have defects in the packaging that make them unmarketable.

[9]This is a project that aims to provide financial aid to households in several problematic areas. Examples are related to housing expenditure, work (e.g. training, renting premises for business, work equipment), health care and debt. The Family Fund is a service that acts as an umbrella for others, like the Emporium.

[10]"Capodarco" is a social cooperative of disabled people that produces and sells egg pasta and donates part of its production to the Emporium.

contribution to the debate regarding social inclusion income, part of which was subsequently included in a legislative measure.

At the local level, the current economic situation with the resulting fragility in the supply of employment and the lack of a collaborative relationship with public institutions limits the effects of the Emporium in terms of capabilities. This, therefore, intensifies the risk of not being able to go beyond the action of merely meeting food needs. Indeed, the research shows the role of local public institutions restricted to the provision of public buildings (requalification of disused properties), and to the provision of lines of credit, for example, the regional tender for anti-poverty projects named "Un taglio alla povertà".

One complaint expressed is the absence of serious social planning in Rome, and the prevalence of a relationship based on delegation rather than subsidiarity: "*While in other cities, the Emporium is a project managed jointly by Caritas with the municipal council, the Provincial council,* etc. … *in Rome it is exclusively a Caritas project*" (Caritas Secretary in Rome).

The lack of synergy with local public institutions is also intertwined with a lack of human resources taking care of the community's needs. For example, there are insufficient social workers and they are unprepared for the community's needs: "*Our feeling is that social workers see the Emporium as yet another obligation. In fact, it shouldn't be an extra commitment, but an extra resource they can use for helping people*" (Emporium's coordinator in "Trionfale").

5.2 Barcelona: The Solidarity Card

While in Rome there is a fragile role for the local public institutions, in Barcelona there is a very different social context that has resulted from the effects of the economic crisis on unskilled workers. The rise in unemployment and the increase in the cost of housing have led to a strong synergy between collective actions of solidarity and local public institutions.

In Barcelona, the municipal council plays a key role in the development of anti-poverty and food security action by cooperating with collective initiatives. Some social issues, such as energy poverty,[11] housing and child poverty, have become part of the political agenda of the local government in Barcelona. This is especially since, under

---

[11]Energy poverty is defined as a condition in which people cannot afford to pay for electricity, water and gas. According to the data provided by the Municipality of Barcelona (source: "El Periodico dell'Ayuntamento"), in 2015, 10% of the city's households and, in general, 750,000 people in Catalonia, experienced a state of energy poverty. Catalan Law 24/2015 prohibits private companies from interrupting the supply of domestic utilities for economic reasons. Companies are required to contact social services instead.

Mayor Ada Colau,[12] people from social movements have started to be part of the local administrative institutions (Alberich, 2016). Alongside a monitoring effort by the municipal council on how inequalities are structured in the different districts of Barcelona, there is a "Citizenship Pact for the Social Inclusion Strategy 2016/2020".[13]

According to the report "Economic situation of the City of Barcelona for the Commission of Economy and Finance" (2016), drafted by the Municipality of Barcelona, two main aspects emerge. On the one hand, the rising gross domestic product: in fact, in Catalonia, it increased by +3.4% in 2015, the highest percentage in the last nine years. On the other hand, inequalities are increasing and creating significant differences between the various districts of Barcelona.

Social exclusion seems to be concentrated in certain areas of Barcelona: the areas in the east of the city, along the Besos River (Nou Barris, St'Andreu, St'Martì), and those in the Old Town (Raval, and Barrio Gotico).

"*The richest neighbourhoods have a household net income 4–5 times higher than the poorest ones*" (Director of the Social Rights Area of Barcelona City Hall). Income poverty also entails health inequality: "*In Barcelona, the life expectancy in rich neighbourhoods is around 85 years, while in the poorest it is 75 years, a ten-year gap*" (Ibid.).

The synergy between public institutions and collective actions of solidarity has deep historical roots in the "Asociaciónes de vecinos" (Neighbourhood Associations), established at the end of the dictatorship. From a locus of protest, these movements continued gradually demanding the rights of citizens, through increasingly active participation within local public institutions. Initially, the public institutions accepted the social ferment which came from the bottom, but over time a gradual disconnect set in. Indeed, in the 1970 s, while parties used to have a vertical structure of dialogue and connection with the community, this link gradually disappeared. Under Ada Colau's administration, this interconnected local-based communication has been re-established.

In order to describe this transformative process,[14] it can be argued that, since the 1970s, there has been an evolution in the nature of the collective actions of solidarity, which has gone through three main stages. The first dates back to the 1970s, when the Asociaciónes de vecinos constituted a protest initiative directed at public infrastructure (roads and schools). The second in 2003–2004, when collective initiatives were aimed at protecting Barcelona from urban projects, which were inconsistent with the "human scale" of the city's planning. The third and last one came in 2011, when there was a

[12]A well-known activist for housing rights, and organizer of the platform that brings people together under housing eviction in Barcelona.

[13]Founded in 2006 with more than 400 entities including institutions, public and private associations. The 400 members draw up a shared project to tackle poverty, defining guidelines on which ad hoc *commissions* are created.

[14]Researcher IGOP, Universitat Autonoma de Barcelona, interview.

radical change in the nature of collective actions. The change was marked by a transition from protest to more involved action, including providing food to people in need, urban allotment schemes, and cooperatives for the self-management of food supply.

The rise in these types of initiatives was not particularly seen with the financial crisis of 2008, but appeared with the Indignados Movement,[15] which conveyed the idea that indignation had to be translated into concrete actions at the local level. The synergy between local public institutions and collective actions of solidarity also takes the same normative approach. This approach aims to reduce poverty and social exclusion not only by offering charitable measures, but also by proactively reducing inequalities.

The research, in fact, revealed cross-cutting interest—shared by various social actors—in a citizenship income provided by the City of Barcelona (on which, it seems, the municipal council is working), to provide an income to effectively meet the needs of citizens.

From the perspective of an analysis of poverty in the context of expanding people's agency, food insecurity is an issue that is disconnected from food waste.[16] The basic idea is that, since food waste is an intrinsic problem of the production system, it needs a solution from businesses[17] themselves. Food security, on the other hand, requires policies to guarantee the right to food, the right to high-quality food. Here, there is a strong link to food sovereignty[18] and, consequently, to the international peasant movement *La* Via *Campesina.*[19]

---

[15]Also known as Movement 15 M. It was a protest movement, formed in Spain in 2011, against austerity measures.

[16]The collective initiatives which adopt this perspective in Barcelona, which consider that the poor should not be fed the leftovers of large-scale production (also because they are of low quality) include, for example: *Xarxa dei Consumi Solidari*, *Veterinaros sin Fronteras* (NGO), Caritas and the Municipality's Solidarity Card project, and the *Assemblea d'aturats de Barcelona.* The latter is a group of unemployed people who, in the Nou Barris neighbourhood (one of the neighbourhoods with the highest unemployment rate), aim to ensure the self-sufficiency and food autonomy of neighbourhood residents through urban gardens and a commitment to ruralize some areas of Barcelona.

[17]Linking the problem of food insecurity to food waste raises a basic contradiction. For example, consider the "Gran Recapte d'Aliments" in Spain, the campaign that invites consumers to buy an extra product at the supermarket and donate it to food banks. People are invited to buy more and, therefore, the production system is stimulated even more. Thus, it contributes to waste, intensifying consumption and production (Gascon and Montagut, 2015).

[18]Food sovereignty means "*The right of peoples to healthy and culturally appropriate food produced through ecologically sound and sustainable methods, and their right to define their own food and agricultural systems*" (Nyéléni Declaration, Mali, Forum on Food Sovereignty, 2007).

[19]Founded in 1993 in Mons (Belgium). La Via Campesina represents small and medium farmers internationally and believes sustainable agriculture can be a tool for promoting dignity and social justice.

The food security approach, as defined in terms of empowerment and dignity, and the interdependence of collective initiatives and local public institutions, are what characterise both the *Estratègia d'Impuls de la Política Alimentària* (Strategy for Promoting Food Policy) and the Solidarity Card project.

In 2013, inspiration for Solidarity Card came from a project called "Carta Equa" (Ethical Card) by the Italian Caritas in Milan, and by the desire of the municipal council and Caritas in Barcelona to find alternative projects to tackle food insecurity.

"*We wanted to find a way to help people in a dignified way (…) leaving them the freedom to choose what to eat, the freedom to buy fresh products*" (Municipality Solidarity Card coordinator).

"*We did not like the Emporium of Solidarity project because it is a place for the poor. Whereas we wanted a project that considered the poor as the same as other people. We wanted them to continue shopping in the place they did it before, to buy what they wanted and when they wanted*" (Caritas Solidarity Card coordinator).

Solidarity Card works to guarantee people's freedom of choice, paying attention to their different nutritional and relational needs. In fact, the idea behind the project is that people can continue to buy from merchants with whom they have built a trusting relationship over time, and above all, not change their diet. Solidarity Card combines autonomy, human dignity and the right to high-quality food, with support for local development.

The Card project intends to be an ambassador for a change in thinking, that does not look at the "poor" as people unable to exercise the faculty of choice, but as people able to define their own needs. This change in mindset, however, meets the reluctance of those who are used to understanding food aid merely as the distribution of meals and, therefore, as a means to simply "give" food to people in need.

"*People prefer to give food items to the poor rather than money because, that way, they can control and decide what people need. When social workers tell me that with Solidarity Card people waste money on alcohol,* etc.... *I share the example of the card used for refugees in Lebanon. There is an interesting United Nations video showing a man who, after 4 years, goes shopping again and, on the way from his home to the neighbourhood shop, he thinks about his shopping list. He makes a shopping list, as we all do when we go to the supermarket. With that credit card he supports the small shops in the neighbourhood and, therefore, the owners of the small shops can continue to sell and avoid becoming poor*" (Caritas Solidarity Card coordinator).

In order to get Solidarity Card, people must contact social services. After examining the personal and household situation (family members, income and expenditures), social workers can decide whether to assign them a Solidarity Card and define the amount and the duration of the aid. The card is one of the building blocks of a complex system of social measures designed to help people overcoming their difficulties through different kinds of support, such as: free legal counselling; Spanish courses for foreigners; intermediary support between the banks and the citizens; rent and mortgage payments;

anti-violence centres for women who are victims of abuse; job placement assistance[20]; and financial support for the payment of household bills.

Solidarity Card is an example of a sense of "social co-responsibility" towards those who are living in a socially excluded situation. This is a co-responsibility that Caritas and the municipal council aim to intensify and extend through a project that allows people -who shop with their own money- to donate a certain percentage to recharge Solidarity Cards. In doing so, they enable other people to continue shopping in their own supermarket. In this way, the practice of "individual freedom" (in this case, going shopping), is linked to the exercise of "solidarity" in enhancing "social responsibility".

Social solidarity takes the form of a collective action that results from the synergy between collective initiatives of solidarity and local public institutions. Thus, a network emerges as an exchange of knowledges and practices at both local and national levels. This leads to cooperative action that strengthens the capability for voice through measures that address the structural conditions that underlie a state of poverty. The *Citizenship Pact for the Social Inclusion Strategy 2016/2020* and the "*Estratègia d'Impuls de la Política Alimentària 2016-2019*", are examples of a collective and institutional commitment, which act directly on the labour supply and on the social guarantees linked to the citizenship income.

5.3 Athens: Kipoda's Solidarity Kitchen

The impacts of the economic crisis -combined with austerity measures- have taken on a more severe form in Greece, leading to a worsening of living conditions (Huliarias, 2015; Matsaganis, 2014). The increase in unemployment, the drastic reduction in incomes (Perez and Matsaganis, 2018) and the consequent increase in inequalities, have lead to an inability to meet basic needs, such as food and health care. This situation of deprivation increased exponentially when combined with shortages in the supply of medicines,[21] cases of deliberate HIV infection in order to gain access to the welfare state subsidy (WHO, 2013), and the humanitarian crisis linked to the arrival of refugees.

The social context is marked by deep deprivations, in which the absence of the Central State[22] is counterbalanced by the action of local public institutions (Sotiropoulos,

[20]The social services of the Municipality use the LABORA platform, which helps people find a job and training courses..

[21]Fearing the insolvency of Greece, pharmaceutical companies frequently disrupt the supply of certain drugs. The shortage of medicines, even in public hospitals, has led to a reliance on solidarity pharmacies that receive donated drugs.

[22]Whose social action is hampered by the fiscal consolidation imposed by the official creditors TROIKA (European Commission - European Central Bank—International Financial Fund).

2014), shipowners' foundations, and collective actions of solidarity with formal and informal structures.[23] Actions entirely based on the fulfilment of basic needs (LIVEWHAT, 2016): distribution of clothes and medicines, free medical visits, community social soup kitchens and support for migrants/refugees.

The activities of NGOs and basic livelihood structures (coordinated by the Municipality) are supported by the European funds (ESPA) for social activities.[24]

It is within this context, that the activities of Kipoda take place. Kipoda (*Kinissi Politon Dytikis Athinas*) the acronym of "Citizens' Movement of Western Athens",[25] founded in 2000, has its headquarters in Peristeri.[26] Over the years, Kipoda has modified its organisational structure, adapting it to the needs of citizens.

In 2012, under the pressure of the devastating effects of the economic crisis, Kipoda was transformed from a "voluntary service association" engaged in blood donation campaigns and the organisation of cultural events, into a non-governmental organisation with facilities and services to help people. Indeed, Kipoda's main services are: the Solidarity Kitchen, the *pantopolio* (the solidarity shop), the solidarity pharmacy and the social services. Beneficiaries have to choose whether to use the *pantopolio* or the Kitchen, while the pharmacy and the social services are available to everyone.

---

[23]Despite the rise -over the last decade- of numerous initiatives, the literature confirms the severe weakness of Greek civil society and explains it with historical and structural references (Huliaras, 2015). According to Sotiropoulos' reconstruction (2014, p. 17), the fact that a strong civil society did not develop in Greece during the 20th century can be traced back to the centralizing role of the State and political parties. The fact that the Regime of the Colonels, which lasted from 1967 to 1974, was not overthrown "from below" (through social mobilization), reduced the opportunities for the development of a civil society.

In the summer of 1974, dictatorship gave way to democracy practically overnight. As a result, there was no time or political space available for action or the development of social initiatives other than political parties. Following the dictatorship, Greek society became heavily politicised, parties catalysed public attention and monopolised social regulation.

Indeed, after 1974, left-wing parties (especially PASOK) founded trade unions and exerted a strong influence on social movements (students and women)..

[24]The AP (Partnership Agreement for the Development Framework) 2014–2020, is the main strategic plan for growth in Greece, in terms of social cohesion and sustainable development, and it is supported by resources from the European Structural and Investment Funds (EIF funds) of the European Union.

[25]The western area of Athens is historically the poorest. For example, some areas of Peristeri, the oldest ones, still have low residential buildings, which belonged to Greek refugees who escaped from Turkey.

[26]The fourth largest municipality in Greece, with almost 600,000 inhabitants, who are mainly from the middle class.

Access to Kipoda's services is subject to proof of certain income requirements: beneficiaries must have a net income below/equal to 3,500 euros per year.[27] In addition to income, other conditions are taken into consideration, such as the composition of the family, home ownership, expenditures (including on health care) and debt obligations. Thus, once it understands people's problems and needs, Kipoda's social service acts as a mediator, directing people to the proper support services, by connecting them to the public employment agency (OAED) or other non-governmental organisations. Unlike other social practices, Kipoda has not introduced time limits for the use of its services, thereby expressing a willingness to support people as long as their condition requires it.

In 2012, when Kipoda began to deal with the effects of the crisis, its work was centred around multiple structures (in addition to those already mentioned) and was characterised by the presence of a dormitory for the homeless, an office for administrative procedures and a "time bank". Using a virtual currency called "TEM", the time bank gave rise to thousands of exchanges (of clothes, furniture and private lessons).[28]

This was the structure of Kipoda until 2017. Later, changes in the conditions and management of the ESPA European funds, forced Kipoda to reduce both the number of assistance services and the number of paid staff (from 14 to 9).[29] Critically, 2017 is an important date, because it marks a sort of watershed, with effects on the structure and effectiveness of Kipoda's intervention. Until 2017, the Central State was in charge of the management of European funds, allocating them directly to social organisations.

Afterwards, European funds from the Ministry of Labour began going to the regions, which then transfer them to the municipalities, and finally, the municipalities allocate the funds to collective actions of solidarity, and to the basic livelihood structures coordinated by the municipal council itself. With the increase in the number of initiatives supported, the funds, for each of these organisations have been reduced, resulting in staff cuts and lowering the economic parameters for accessing Kipoda's support structures. In fact, the income threshold for beneficiaries has gone from 5,000 euros a year, to 3,500 euros (for a single person).

In addition, there has also been an impact on the role of collective actions of solidarity and their field of action: "*Of the 64 initiatives financed through the ESPA Fund, 59 belong to the municipalities, while the remaining organisations mostly deal with refugees. Therefore, the municipalities are entirely responsible for managing other social issues*" (Director of Kipoda).

---

[27] A couple (wife and husband or mother and child) 5,500 euros; for three people, 7,500 euros; for four people, 8,500 euros; for five people, 12,500 euros.

[28] Two employees were paid to manage the online exchange platform. The platform had 600 residents from Peristeri and 400 from other municipalities.

[29] Kipoda operates through paid staff and 15 volunteers who take care of the administrative, communication and logistics side of activities.

The interviews showed not only how important European funding is to support Kipoda's activities, but also the inefficiencies associated with the management of these funds:

"*From February 2017 to May 2017, we worked as volunteers, because we had to wait for the Region to decide on the distribution of the new ESPA funding. We continued to run the pharmacy because Peristeri is one of the largest municipalities in Greece and so there are many people in need*" (Solidarity Pharmacy coordinator).

Outlined here are the structure and services of Kipoda. The solidarity pharmacy works like a normal pharmacy. The parameters required are more flexible compared to those required for the Kitchen and *pantopolio.* This is because many people no longer have medical insurance or, even if they do have it, cannot afford part of the cost of medicines[30]: "*Even though this can be as low as, say, 2 or 3 euros*" (Solidarity Pharmacy coordinator).

For some medications, a doctor's prescription is required. In situations where people cannot wait for medication or to get onto a hospital waiting list for a free visit, or are unable to pay ten euros for a private visit, they can contact voluntary doctors' associations (e.g. KIBE[31]).

Every month, the solidarity pharmacy distributes medicines to 230 beneficiaries, mostly men over the age of 60. The most prescribed drugs are for chronic diseases (heart and respiratory) and anti-depressants and psychiatric medications. The drugs in the solidarity pharmacy are donated by private individuals and, therefore, by people who have medicines at home that they no longer use.[32] When a donation is received, the people in charge of the pharmacy check the state of the drugs, and then distribute them to people in single doses, according to their needs.[33]

Kipoda named the solidarity shop "*pantopolio*", a nostalgic word which comes from "*pantopolia*", the little neighbourhood shops that were widespread in the 1950s, and sold everything from foodstuffs to household items.

"*We decided to give it this name to remind our beneficiaries that pantopolio where they can get essentials. So it is not like a supermarket where people can get lots of things*" (Director of Kipoda).

People can go to *pantopolio* once a month and get a box prepared for them (with products donated by the Municipality, supermarkets, private individuals, shipowners'

---

[30]Health insurance covers part of the cost.

[31]Medical prescriptions from these organizations are not electronic and, therefore, can only be accepted in solidarity pharmacies.

[32]Only a few organizations (for example, the non-governmental organization "Alma Zois" which deals with cancer patients) are authorized to distribute cancer drugs.

[33]Kipoda's drugs are also donated by pharmaceutical companies who decide which drugs should be donated and in what quantities. Basically, their donations cover three to four months of the activity of the solidarity pharmacy.

associations), which generally covers basic needs for one or two weeks. About 270 families are beneficiaries of *pantopolio*. Previously this number was 600, but the access criteria are more restrictive owing to the new management of ESPA funds.

"*Welcome to Greece, Welcome to Hell! (..) This is the eighth year of crisis for Greece*" (Director of Kipoda).

Another service by Kipoda is the Solidarity Kitchen. Unlike *pantopolio*, the Kitchen distributes meals once a day, six days a week. It opens at 10.45 am and closes at 1.30 pm. Kipoda takes note of the meals delivered, which might be ready-made or require cooking. The Kitchen only works as a distribution point, where beneficiaries go to collect meals for themselves and their families. Every day, 52 families (totalling 111 people) get their meals, while another 85 families benefit only two or three times a week.

Each beneficiary[34] is given a specific time of day to collect meals, in order to avoid long queues, thus safeguarding the dignity of people from having to show everyone how vulnerable they are. The products of the Kitchen come from restaurants, the Navy cafeteria, supermarkets, the Bourume[35] organisation and *laiki* farmers' markets.[36] Donated food is checked and divided into individual portions.[37]

"*If we can, we try to give portions that can be enough for the evening. (...) We don't only give cooked portions, but also try to supplement them with products donated from the supermarket such as cheese, yoghurt, ready-made salads,* etc. *When the food arrives, we check what state it is in (by smell, by eyesight), but we cannot force donors to put labels on donated food*" (Food Distribution Coordinator).

As far as donations are concerned, it is necessary to highlight two aspects: the first is that, since the crisis, supermarkets donate less because they are ordering in smaller quantities, knowing they will be selling less. The second aspect is that Greece has no legislative framework that encourages donations; in fact, "*companies actually pay taxes even on donated food*" (Director of Bourume). This makes the work of organisations, such as Kipoda more complicated, because their food support is completely based on donations.

---

[34]In order to gain access to the Solidarity Kitchen, people must not only meet the economic criteria for access, but must also sign a protocol, by which, they undertake to respect the appointments, to take what the kitchen offers, and not to communicate to third parties what meals they have received, so as not to create conflicts between the beneficiaries.

[35]Bourume, which means "We can", was founded in 2012 as a reaction to the social oxymoron that sees, on the one hand, an abundance and waste of food and, on the other, a growing number of people in situations of food insecurity. Bourume connects the donors with the beneficiaries (e.g. Orthodox Church canteens, municipal social services, refugee associations, organizations with social aims).

[36]The price of fruit and vegetables is much lower in the *laiki* than in supermarkets. At the end of the working day, *laiki* producers donate their unsold products.

[37]Kipoda prepares individualized menus, paying attention to allergies and intolerances, as well as the availability of a refrigerator for storing food and/or stoves for heating and cooking in the beneficiaries' home.

The state of emergency affects the structure of Kipoda, shaping a counteraction entirely focused on the urgency of offering people an immediate response to their needs. In this perspective, there is a lack of attention towards a more structured analysis of food insecurity, focusing on autonomy and food quality. In addition, on the one hand, there is an acknowledgement of the contribution and commitment of local governments and their role as intermediaries with food donors, but on the other, there is a conflicting relationship with public institutions.

"*The institutions seem more inclined to obstruct us. They wanted us to close the solidarity pharmacy, because they say medicines are cheap so we're not needed*" (Director of Kipoda).

Moreover, there is no legislative framework to support the activities of NGOs. NGOs are subject to the same laws as businesses, and there are also strict regulations on volunteering. The competitive relationship between Kipoda and local public institutions for the management of ESPA funds, together with the dense network of cooperation with other collective solidarity initiatives, essentially result in a weak capability for voice. The latter seems to be trapped in a "charity" mindset, where only basic needs are met, essentially as a continued reaction to an emergency. Indeed, the synergy between Kipoda and the third sector and institutional context, is only focused on stepping up donations of food, clothing and medicines. There is no collective action -as an expression of social solidarity- to address the root causes of deprivation.

6 Emporium of Solidarity, Solidarity Card and Solidarity Kitchen: The Impact of Social Solidarity in Terms of Strengthening Beneficiaries' Agency

6.1 Rome: The Emporium of Solidarity

The beneficiaries of the Emporium of Solidarity are households with minors. Their life path is characterised by a set of initial endowments in which the native family, sometimes working class and sometimes lower middle class, have a low-medium level of education (i.e. primary and lower secondary school). With some differentiation, the beneficiaries show an ability to convert their initial endowment of resources into a medium-high level of education (high school and university). In some cases, the "unfavourable" starting conditions have resulted in a limited freedom of choice for their educational path, due to the economic difficulties faced by their native family.

Despite a medium-high level of education, training pathways and previous work experience (as workers, employees or small entrepreneurs), most encounter increasing difficulties in achieving the substantive freedom to choose work that is decent (ILO, 1999) and in line with their life plans. In fact, beneficiaries show a compromised agency, with the consequent emergence of adaptive choices towards jobs that do not meet their preferences, poorly paid and often irregular.

The main factor that alters the conversion of initial tangible/intangible resources into actual freedoms is an individual's social and institutional profile (age, health and gender-related). For example, it is difficult for over-50-year-olds, who have lost their jobs often for health reasons (e.g. illness or work-related accidents) during adulthood, to find a new job. In addition, there are also gender differences. In fact, both Italian and foreign women only have sporadic or temporary jobs, limited to caring for the elderly or housekeeping. Women have difficulty finding a job that allows them to take care of their children. Thus, social conversion factors emerge as very limiting.

"I do some work but it's not much, that's also because my little daughter goes to school near home while the older one's school is further away and I have to take her. It's

D. Bernaschi, *Collective Actions of Solidarity against Food Insecurity*, RaumFragen: Stadt – Region – Landschaft, https://doi.org/10.1007/978-3-658-31375-3_6

hard to find a job from 10:30/11:00 onwards. I do housekeeping work" (Woman, foreign, 36 years old).

"*I've been unemployed since last July. I earned 500/600 euros but half of it was spent on the babysitter, so I preferred to quit that job*" (Woman, Italian, 44 years old).

The main drivers of deprivation derive from a compromised conversion mechanism, involving not only the loss of employment, but also—especially for women— "divorce" (often the epilogue of a violent relationship), which leads to the loss of a family support network.

"*I'm alone and I have a little girl. I can't find a job*" (Woman, foreign, 39 years old).

"*The most important choice I've made in life was to break away from my husband because he was violent and I was afraid he would kill my daughter*—she becomes emotional-. *Even though, I was left alone and have many difficulties, I think it was the best choice! I couldn't live in fear anymore*" (Woman, foreign, 42 years old).

The particular situations experienced by people were not met with adequate re-integration of "lost" entitlements by public institutions. Thus, the issue relates to institutional conversion factors: insufficient pensions, unemployment benefits precluded by the irregular nature of work, and strict requirements for access to minimum income measures (for example, the Support for Active Inclusion—SIA). This leads beneficiaries to turn to the family support network and to the Emporium of Solidarity.

"*I only have the Emporium and a* retirement *of € 220 per month*" (Man, Italian, 75 years old).

"*I had applied to the SIA which came out in November but I didn't reach the minimum score of 45 points…I got about 38 points…the choice of the Emporium was a bit forced, because this way for 5 months I can at least provide for the needs of my children – napkins, wipes and biscuits – and so at least I don't have to think about that*" (Man, Italian, 50 years old).

Regarding the impact of the initiative in terms of agency, the Emporium by freeing the beneficiaries from the worry of food expenses, allows them to focus on other expenses.

"*It's enough help..so I can pay the bills, for school*" (Woman, foreign, 36 years old).

Nevertheless, the limited quantity and variety of the Emporium's offering (based on donations), generates important constraints both on nutritional and food-related relational choices. Therefore, it is lacking the social value of food linked to conviviality.

"*We only do a limited amount of shopping at the Emporium, it is not possible to share with anyone outside the family. In fact, my husband's parents bring us meals they have already cooked*" (Woman, foreign, 42 years old).

Integration of food expenditure is particularly necessary when there are different dietary customs (especially given the presence of foreign beneficiaries) and nutritional needs:

"*I am from Bangladesh and when I can't find something here, because we eat a lot of rice, I buy it somewhere else. I buy fish and meat somewhere else*" (Woman, foreign, 28 years old).

"*I am lactose-intolerant, to margarine and so on (...) So, the shopping I do here is only for my mother and my brother and if I don't find anything, I don't eat*" (Woman, Italian, 40 years old).

The people interviewed appreciate the opportunity of being able to choose and buy food -albeit circumscribed-, because there is a margin of autonomy that does not exist with other forms of food aid, like food parcels and the social canteens.

Some people point out that the scarcity of food, makes it impossible to include people outside of the family in moments of conviviality. Others, claim they have not given up the practice, because they live in contexts where food is "shared". In this case, the chance to keep maintaining social ties and adopting practices of conviviality, are linked to cultural traits and the possibility of having neighbourly relationships. Women, in particular, are careful and more inclined to include people outside the family during meals.

The Emporium is just one of the many services made available by Caritas with the aim of strengthening agency. In fact, the beneficiaries state that they also use the centre for psychological support, the legal assistance centre for divorce matters, and receive aid for paying household utilities and rent. Moreover, although Caritas' support also extends to job seeking, it remains limited to the care of the elderly and the home. This, in turn, fosters adaptive choices in women.

"*I am enrolled in several Caritas centres for finding work... but it's difficult because the jobs they offer require a 24/24 h commitment and I can't, I have my 14-year-old daughter and two 5 and 7-year-old daughters of my sister*" (Woman, foreign, 43 years old).

Although the normative approach is to strengthen the agency of beneficiaries, the lack of collaboration with local public institutions and the "free" -but circumscribed- access to food resources, risk altering its actual impact on the beneficiaries' substantive freedoms, and on their ability to aspire to change and design new life plans. The Emporium does not seem to provide sufficient strength for this projection of change.

6.2 Barcelona: The Solidarity Card

In Barcelona, the majority of beneficiaries are Spanish women aged over 55, single or divorced, with minors. In most cases, their life path is characterised by coming from working class families with a primary level of education.

The structure of the initial endowments combined with the action of specific conversion factors, have conditioned their substantive freedom to receive an education. Indeed, the beneficiaries present a heterogeneous level of education that varies between primary school and university degree level. The limitations and achievements in terms of education have conditioned the number of capabilities available, leading them to be employed as housekeepers or as caretakers of the elderly, or as self-employed individuals and office workers. In some cases, the prevalence of compromised agency is at the root of choices—in the employment sector—evidencing an adaptive situation.

The main drivers that alter the conversion of tangible and intangible resources into freedoms and opportunities, which in turn, lead to deprivation, are personal and social in nature. Personal deprivation is linked to health problems which, in many cases, are associated with the loss of employment. Examples of social deprivation include shortages in jobs, or high housing costs which force people to share their homes with friends and tourists. In fact, the inability to pay high rents prevents single-parent families and people over 55, from enjoying the freedom of intimacy and their own living space, forcing them to adopt solutions involving sharing and, in some cases, protest (i.e. occupation of housing).

"*I live in another lady's house, I help her with her children and, in return, she lets me live there without paying rent. I don't work and have no income at all, so I couldn't afford to pay the rent*" (Woman, Spanish, 58 years old).

"*The apartment costs 900 euros a month but since I can't afford that rent, I share a house with two other women*" (Woman, Spanish, 45 years old).

"*800 euros for the rent but I don't have a job so I'm now occupying the house with a group of friends*" (Woman, Colombian, 53 years old).

After losing their jobs, the interviewees received different forms of support from the displaced entitlements from the Central State and the *Generalitat de Cataluña*, moving, therefore, from unemployment benefits to RAI[1] or PIRMI.[2] In addition to these measures, there is also other aids from the Municipality of Barcelona for households (to tackle energy poverty) and for rent. The latter is provided by the *Habitatge de l'Ajuntament de Barcellona* for housing rights. The research shows how far the interviewees rely on public support in order to overcome economic difficulties.

Despite the fact that there is a wide network of public aids, its fragmented nature and the lack of coordination, place limits on its effectiveness, leaving gaps which are partly made up by the Solidarity Card.

The beneficiaries have highlighted the advantages of the Card in terms of the expansion of their agency, often comparing it with other aid measures, such as soup kitchens or food parcels. Beneficiaries who go to the social soup kitchen or get food parcels have no choice, receiving what others have prepared and decided for them. Therefore, the provided support does not perfectly reflect their own needs and preferences.

"*Before I go assistance from the Church, only going to the social canteen is not the same as using the Solidarity Card. I'm Muslim, so I cannot eat everything, and at the canteen, food is the same for everyone, while with the Card I can go to the supermarket and buy whatever I want*" (Woman, Moroccan, 35 years old).

---

[1]Inclusion Active Income (RAI), a national measure aimed at the re-employment of people aged over 45, in long-term unemployment and with dependent family members.

[2]Cataluña's Minimum Inclusion Income, a subsidy for those aged between 25 and 65.

Moreover, food parcels contain standardised and long-life food, whereas the Solidarity Card allows people not only to decide autonomously what to eat, but also to have a diversified diet, eating fresh products.

"*As soon as they gave me the Card, the first thing I did was to go to the supermarket and shop for 30 euros. I bought everything I needed, because I had nothing at home. I bought the basic necessities and also products for lactose-intolerant people*" (Woman, Spanish, 65 years old).

"*With the Solidarity Card I buy meat, milk, pasta, vegetables, fruit (…) I also buy bread, because gluten-free bread costs a lot (…) and now with the Card I can buy it*" (Woman, Spanish, 55 years old).

The nutrition of beneficiaries has improved with the Solidarity Card. Moreover, it allows them to concentrate on other expenses and no longer be anxious about food resources.

"*So many things have changed since I've been using the Card. It's taken a weight off me, it has taken away the stress of not being able to do the shopping. When I didn't have the Card, in the evening I had nothing to eat, and in the end, I only had milk with cereal. Now, instead, I can take more care of my diet and have a varied diet. The most important thing is that my daughter eats well. My daughter is 14 years old and it is important to me that she has a balanced diet. The important thing is that, she can eat well now, and thanks to the Solidarity Card I can eat well, too*" (Woman, Spanish, 55 years old).

Shopping free of charge in any way encourages a sense of irresponsibility on the part of the interviewees, who are committed to making the most of the help provided by the municipal council. They shop, for example, in the cheapest supermarkets (e.g. Mercadona and Bon Preu), and often choose special offers. The Solidarity Card is not only used to buy meat, fish, milk, fruit and vegetables, but also for hygiene and household products.

Although the interviewees highlighted the importance of the Card in ensuring autonomous choice and a healthy and diversified diet, especially for their children (this is the main concern for the women interviewed), they complain about their reliance on external help. For this reason, the interviewees look for training programmes that can ensure their re-employment, and also show a strong ability to create new life opportunities, especially foreign interviewees who are sometimes victims of sexual discrimination.

"*I left Russia because I am homosexual and therefore preferred to live in Europe, in more tolerant countries. I married a bisexual Austrian girl; we were planning to have a child together. So I moved to Vienna but, after a year, the relationship with this woman ended because of a series of problems. I lost all the privileges I had and, after a year, I found myself alone in a country that was not mine. It was not easy to find myself alone and start all over again*" (Man, Russian, 56 years old).

"*I gave up the possibility of working at the university in Morocco because I preferred to live my sexuality peacefully, living in a country that was more free and respectful of my sexual preferences (…) I fell in love with my cousin who lived in Barcelona and, therefore, I left everything to follow her here. Once here in Barcelona, I realised that she was an escort and, therefore, we each went our separate ways. Observing some lifeguards, I realised that I could swim better than them, so I asked for information and that's how my career began here in Barcelona*" (Woman, Moroccan, 35 years old).

The use of the Solidarity Card is part of a process that supports the beneficiaries' claim for autonomy and independence, through employment and training assistance.

"*I would suggest to the Municipality to focus on helping people find a job. The Municipality is helping me find a job. I also do training courses for the computer. They explained to me how to look for a job and how to write a CV*" (Man, Moroccan, 55 years old).

"*Social services have helped me a lot! They put me in contact with a care centre run by nuns for rehabilitation and they also helped me financially to pay for classes to become a nurse*" (Woman, Moroccan, 35 years old).

The Solidarity Card strengthens the beneficiaries' freedom of agency, on the one hand, by targeting nutrition in the short-term, promoting free choice and ensuring a diversified and quality diet; on the other hand, in line with a long-term perspective, it promotes support for employment and new professional integration (facilitated by training programmes). All this is carried out, by paying attention to the preferences and skills of the beneficiaries.

6.3 Athens: Kipoda's Solidarity Kitchen

In Athens, the majority of the Solidarity Kitchen's beneficiaries are unmarried people, living with their native relatives, or divorced women with children. They are people with either a working class or an entrepreneurial background. While their parents are characterised by a primary education, the beneficiaries generally have a high school education.

The economic difficulties of their own native families have limited the freedom of choice, especially in education, affecting their resulting job opportunities. "*My family was very poor* -he became emotional-. *My father was a bricklayer. Immediately after primary school, I started working in the workshop to bring money home and to help my family. I didn't like working in the workshop, I wanted to continue studying and become an electrician*" (Man, Greek, 69 years old).

There are also conversion factors which are personal in nature (e.g. health problems that prevent people from finding a job), and social factors arising from the lack of employment supply and the health care system, which interfere with their effective opportunities/freedoms to obtain valued achievements.

Emerging factors of deprivation include:

- A state of long-term unemployment: "*My last job ended because the company where I worked for 5 years no longer had a job. (...) I have been unemployed for 55 months*" (Man, Greek, 29 years old).

- The presence of temporary, underpaid and paid-off-the-book work: "*For 2 – 3 years, I've been working as a transporter for a pharmaceutical company. I earn 450 euros a month, I work 5 days a week for 8 h a day*" (Man, Greek, 40 years old).
- People over 60 who have lost their jobs in adulthood, find themselves in the situation of being forced to wait for their retirement: "*I should have taken retirement at the age of 57, because I was working on the ships (…) But, having been out of work for so long, I missed this opportunity. I have been unemployed for 67 months*" (Man, Greek, 64 years old).
- The existence of debts with banks and the EFKA (the social security system) by self-employed people: "*I have debts with banks and the EFKA. From an initial debt of 3,000 euros, it has reached 30,000 euros and I'm afraid that they may take my house (…) I had a tobacco shop which I closed in 2013 because of the crisis*" (Woman, 52 years old Greek). "*When I was self-employed, I paid 450 euros a month for insurance and social security contributions (…)I haven't paid any for two years (…). I also owe 100,000 euros to the banks, but the banks don't bother me because they're waiting for my pension*" (Man, Greek, 62 years old).

Institutional conversion factors also impact beneficiaries' freedoms. In fact, the interviewees turn to Kipoda's Solidarity Kitchen due to the lack of public integration of lost entitlements (partly because of the irregular state of their employment), or because they are insufficient (e.g. long-term unemployment benefits of 200 euros per month). The weaknesses of the public social system are offset by the key role played by the family of origin. Indeed, the interviews show how crucial the retirement of one's parents is, for coping with growing economic difficulties.

"*I live at my father's house. My father gets a 580 euros pension*" (Man, Greek, 55 years old).

"*Before, my mother's pension was 600 euros and she could help us. Now it's 350 euros and she can't anymore*" (Woman, Greek, 52 years old).

Regarding Kipoda's impact in terms of strengthening their agency, beneficiaries receive not only food aid but also free medicines, as many of them are not covered by insurance.

"*I didn't pay insurance for two years, so I couldn't get free diabetes drugs (…) I had no medicines for diabetes for a long time and I lost sight in one eye (…) In the end, I started using my parents' medicines (…) then I came here to Kipoda*" (Man, Greek, 62 years old).

Kipoda's support also regards the job seeking assistance, working as an intermediary with the public employment office and other departments. "*Kipoda helped me to sign up at the public employment office and get 200 euros a month for long-term unemployment*" (Man, Greek, 69 years old).

The interviewees stated that they voluntarily switched from *pantopolio* to being users of the Solidarity Kitchen. Although *pantopolio* offers more freedom in the choice and preparation of meals, the Solidarity Kitchen enables beneficiaries to save money on ingredients and household utilities (e.g. electricity, gas).

"*We have chosen the Kitchen because it is cheaper, more convenient and because we don't know if we will still have electricity in the future*" (Woman, Greek, 52 years old).

In addition, as one interviewee notes: "*At the Kitchen, I can get ready meals every day (4 portions), while in pantopolio, the food lasted only until the middle of the month*" (Man, Greek, 62 years old).

The Solidarity Kitchen distributes generous meals based mainly on carbohydrates (pasta, bread and "*tiropita*" i.e. a pie filled with vegetables), which generally cover both lunch and dinner. Although meals are plentiful and Kipoda is committed to customizing menus to meet people' needs, there is a scarce food aid variety linked to donations, which therefore requires beneficiaries to integrate it.

"*I am diabetic. The coordinator of Kipoda knows this and tries to adapt the meals, obviously depending on what people donate (...) When I go to the supermarket, I buy (...) milk, yoghurt, and what I need because I have osteoporosis*" (Woman, Greek, 72 years old).

While some interviewees try to combine Kipoda's meals with products on special offer at supermarkets or with fruit and vegetables from the *laiki*, others cannot afford it and complain about the absence of certain products from their diet: "*I don't shop at the supermarket anymore because I can't afford it. I haven't eaten suvlaki* [a meat snack] *and chocolate for 4 years, even though they are cheap, only 2 euros*" (Man, Greek, 46 years old).

The reliance on meals prepared and cooked by other people, causes feelings of shame and embarrassment for the beneficiaries. Instead, they prefer aid systems that can preserve their dignity and autonomy. Specifically, the gender variable explains the social discomfort associated with a lack of family self-sufficiency, especially in relation to the quality of food for their children.

"*I miss cooking, I miss cooking the way I wanted and the food I wanted. I miss, above all, knowing what's inside every single meal: the ingredients, the quality of the ingredients... and this, above all, for my son, I don't know what I'm giving to my son*" (Woman, Greek, 55 years old).

"*I miss cooking, but what I miss most is the feeling of being the one who brings food home for my family*" (Woman, Greek, 46 years old).

"*My son doesn't know I come here to the Kitchen. When he comes home, he finds everything ready in the pot. I don't say anything to him because when he found out that I had got food from the Church, he criticised me*" (Woman, Greek, 55).

"*The voucher is better because I can buy whatever I want*" (Woman, Greek, 55).

Kipoda's ready-made meals which depend on food waste and surpluses in restaurants and supermarkets, are not only insufficient to meet the nutritional needs of the beneficiaries, reducing their independence and self-esteem, but they also diminish the convivial and relational value of food. In fact, the Solidarity Kitchen's food is not enough for sharing with people outside the family. Consequently, some interviewees, especially women, renounce to conviviality, while others keep having it by going to friends and relatives' homes.

Thus, the approach adopted by Kipoda seems to compromise the beneficiaries' agency and, in turn, their autonomy and control over their nutrition. Relying on a choice made outside of one's own will, strongly affects the dimension of self-esteem and substantive freedoms. Although Kipoda's normative approach is aimed at strengthening the agency of beneficiaries, in practice there, appears to be a discrepancy with its actual impact. Indeed, Kipoda's cooperation network with other collective solidarity actions and local public institutions is solely focused on supporting food/clothing/medical donations, with a mindset of meeting basic needs in an emergency condition.

Capabilities-Oriented Initiatives or Mere *Compensation for Shortcomings*: A Comparative Reflection

7

7.1 The Life Trajectories of the Beneficiaries: Shared Enabling and Disabling Factors in Terms of Capabilities

From a comparative perspective, Chapter 7 aims to provide answers to the three key research questions that have given support and structure to the study on food security collective actions of solidarity:

1. What are the main drivers of food insecurity and which are the most affected social groups?
2. What influence does the social and institutional context (in the form of rights, resources and legal channels of access to them) have on the generative process of individual capabilities?
3. What is the impact of the collective actions of solidarity in terms of capabilities?
   - Do they succeed, through a network of collaboration between collective actions of solidarity and local public institutions, in strengthening the capability for voice and expanding individual capabilities?
   - Are they able to strengthen the beneficiaries' agency?
   - Are they *capabilities-oriented* or merely compensating for shortcomings?

To answer these questions, it seems useful to analyse the interviews with the beneficiaries, leaving aside the purely individual dimension. In doing so, this book aims to trace the "common elements" in their life trajectories and highlight the disabling and enabling factors in terms of capabilities. This will make possible to understand how the beneficiaries' substantive freedoms are affected by the support of the collective initiatives.

D. Bernaschi, *Collective Actions of Solidarity against Food Insecurity*, RaumFragen: Stadt – Region – Landschaft, https://doi.org/10.1007/978-3-658-31375-3_7

The research shows that the beneficiaries present a compromised initial endowments status. In the Greek and Italian cases, this condition is characterised by high school drop-out due to economic reasons, and in the Spanish case, by a lack of strong family ties (Granovetter, 1997). These factors tend to complicate the framework of the interviewees' opportunities. These starting conditions give rise to adaptive choices (especially in terms of employment), and to a lack of family network as social capital (Bourdieu, 1985; Zamagni, 1996) with its impact on relational bonds and as network of opportunities (Granovetter, 1997).

In the three different local contexts, the beneficiaries seem speaking the same language in terms of substantive freedoms deprivation. These deprivations triggered mainly by events which restricted their choices and directly affected their well-being.: domestic violence, debts, absence or insufficiency of public income integration measures, unemployment, the prevalence of irregular or temporary jobs, divorce as a relational and economic failure, and finally, social relations compromised by economic difficulties.

Alongside these connections, we find fault lines that are affected by both the characteristics of the different normative and social contexts, and by the presence of beneficiaries with different needs, personal skills and expectations. These faults highlight the different drivers at the origin of food insecurity as a deprivation of capabilities.

In Rome, the main reported disabling factors are: unemployment, which in many cases depends on temporary health conditions; the absence of public measures to support income, especially given the prevalence of irregular and temporary jobs; and the difficulty faced by women in finding a job that would allow them to combine work with family care, especially when divorce emerges as a failure in relational terms.

"*When I decided to split up with my first partner, it was a tough decision, because I was alone in Italy with two children... I was so scared!*" (Foreign woman, 43 years old, Rome).

In Athens, on the other hand, most of the beneficiaries identify the following disabling factors in addition to unemployment: the absence of public income integration measures and the presence of irregular or temporary jobs. Here, divorce emerges as a failure not only in relational terms but also in economic terms.

"*My two ex-husbands do not help me with the children. If you want to get something you have to pay a lawyer and I can't afford one*" (Greek woman, 46 years old, Athens).

In Barcelona, on the other hand, we find other disabling conditions that are linked, on one hand, to the high cost of housing and, on the other, to inadequate public income support measures that do not meet real needs.

"*I am an artist, and people who self-employed like me have to pay 280 euros to social security every month. With the public financial support that I receive, I would not be able to survive and so I have to continue doing off-the-books work*" (Foreign man, 56 years old, Barcelona).

Rome and Athens present many similarities with regard to the events that have led to a strengthening of capabilities. In both cities, in fact, community and family relationships play a crucial role in offering material and relational resources for the empowerment of the beneficiaries. As Lyberaki and Tinios (2014) point out, the family -with its support system- replaces public welfare measures, and the crisis is no longer a matter for the State, but is also a concern whose solution is under the family's responsibility.

Community ties are therefore strengthened by the involvement of collective actions of solidarity, which interact as a relational bond, offering food, psychological and employment support. The collective initiatives act as a driving force for the cohesion of the social fabric, stimulating social solidarity which is seen as co-responsibility.

The element separating the two local contexts is that, while the beneficiaries of the Emporium in Rome demonstrate a reinforcement of their agency (in terms of autonomy and freedom of choice—albeit fictitious—regarding their diet), with its nutritional and cultural implications, this is not the case for Kipoda's beneficiaries. Indeed, thanks to food support, they can breathe a sigh of relief and focus on other issues, such as job seeking. Nevertheless, for most of them, real support comes from their families. The family is the social capital that strengthens the alternative choices available. In Barcelona, we find a diametrically opposite situation, in which the role of the family is replaced by local public institutions, and where food support and the strengthening of beneficiaries agency seem to be the most enabling drivers for the interviewees.

Thus, while in Rome, the Emporium plays an enabling role in the beneficiaries' life trajectories, in Athens it is the family, and in Barcelona it is the synergy between the collective actions of solidarity and the local public institutions.

7.2 "Capabilities-Oriented" or "Compensation for Shortcomings" Initiatives

Rome, Barcelona and Athens are all characterised by the particular structure of their social problems, and by different legal channels to access resources and rights[1], within a framework where local public institutions interact and collaborate with collective actions of solidarity at varying intensity.

The main drivers of food insecurity are unemployment and off-the-books work/temporary/underpaid jobs. In all three contexts, other factors contribute to the state of deprivation, such as: divorce in terms of relational failure, and the difficulties faced by women in finding some jobs opportunities, in the case of Rome; high housing costs, in the case of Barcelona; and debts with banks and EFKA, and divorce as economic and relational failure, in the case of Athens.

[1]In Spain, in all Regions, there is the *Renta Mínima de Inserción* (PIRMI, Minimum Inclusion Income) as the last-resort safety nets. In Greece, after an initial reticence and a phase of experimentation at local level, on 1 February 2017, the State introduced a minimum income scheme at the national level, referred to it as the "*Social Solidarity Income*". In Italy, Law no. 33 of 15/03/2017 introduced the "*Reddito di Inclusione -REI-*" (i.e. the Inclusion Income).

Whereas access to the Solidarity Card is universal, access to Kipoda's Solidarity Kitchen and the Emporium is constrained, owing to a lack of resources, which leads them to invest only in certain people to make the best use of the scarce resources available. Therefore, in the Rome scheme, those selected are people with a good chance of getting out of poverty, whereas in Athens, it is those living in a state of severe deprivation that are chosen.

In addition, all the initiatives have a normative approach that is aimed at expanding the agency of the beneficiaries, through support that goes beyond the distribution of food resources and includes: job seeking assistance, language classes, health and housing assistance, all within a process of social inclusion. Nonetheless, the different structure of the relationship with local public institutions and the way food aid is received, reveal a poor fit with their "capabilities-oriented" aspirations.

Indeed, in Rome, social solidarity takes the form of a network of collaboration to foster capabilities, but only with other collective actions of solidarity. Thus, synergy with local public institutions is lacking. The experience of the Emporium shows that people with different combinations of "capability deprivations" can work together to create strong networks of solidarity. Consider, for example, the way volunteers of the Emporium and social cooperatives (of disabled people or former prisoners), interact with each other and support the activities of the Emporium. In this way, people in need do not become passive recipients of social supports. Instead, they are the active agents who contribute to the innovative approach of the initiative itself, and to the social change in terms of substantive freedoms.

At the same time, however, the particular economic situation and the absence of a collaborative relationship with the institutions, adversely affect the fulfillment of the project's goals and limit its effective impact. Additionally, "donated" food resources to tackle food waste restrict beneficiaries' agency, compromise their nutritional, cultural and relational needs.

Indeed, the Emporium addresses food insecurity, while linking it closely to food waste issue and, in doing so, plays a significant role in the social use of food surpluses. This role is also encouraged by Italian legislation, which provides incentives and bureaucratic simplifications to facilitate donations by companies. At local level, therefore, the Emporium plays a strategic role in terms of circular economy. Indeed, it is an important channel for reducing waste, redistributing resources among those who are deprived, and thus contributing to environmental and social sustainability. In addition, the largest donations received make it possible to help the most socially vulnerable people by including them in social economy networks (for example, cooperatives of disabled people are, in turn, suppliers of the Emporium).

On one hand, it shows an awareness of the sustainability challenge faced by the productive system, on the other hand, it links the resolution of food insecurity to the surpluses generated by the productive system itself. The Emporium has no upstream involvement in the production and distribution models that characterise the economy of waste, but only intervenes in its redistribution.

The organisational limitations of the Emporium include the following: first, a supermarket that can only be used by a few people in need, could encourage some forms of segregation. Second, although it tries to recreate an ordinary environment, in practice, the Emporium interrupts the routine in which people go shopping in neighbourhood shops or supermarkets, where they have established trust-based relationships with retailers. Third, since the Emporium's supplies are linked to donations, they are sometimes not sufficient to meet the different nutritional, cultural and relational needs.

Generally, these considerations make the Emporium *capabilities-oriented*, however, only to the selected beneficiaries target. This capabilities orientation is weakened both by a lack of collaboration with local public institutions and by the limited food resources available.

In Barcelona, the Solidarity Card has emerged as a *capabilities-oriented* initiative that aims to expand beneficiaries agency in two ways. The first is through universal and active access to its services and food resources (available on the market system), and the second is through a network of collaboration, between collective actions of solidarity and local public institutions, focused on enhancing capabilities.

The Solidarity Card can ensure autonomous choice and a diversified food supply for beneficiaries. Thanks to it, people can buy food products that meet their nutritional needs (e.g. products for people with food intolerances, Halal products), continuing their own lifestyle. The Solidarity Card can only be used to purchase food and hygiene products, it does not take into consideration other everyday daily needs such as medicines, clothing and pet food. Moreover, although the idea behind the Card was also to support small traders, in practice, the interviewees actually go to low-cost supermarket (with a clear impact on food quality). In some cases, they complain of not being able to use the Card in neighbourhood markets and shops.

Regarding the access conditions to the Solidarity Card, there are no specific income parameters, or considerations for the return in terms of human capital. Instead, there is an analysis and a plan that are tailored to promote substantive freedoms. The Card is a cornerstone in a wider support network for the beneficiary, which is intended to encourage a growth path through, for example, job seeking support (e.g. the LABORA service) and training programmes for re-inclusion into the job market, that is specific to individual life plans. The Card covers specific situations where people are looking for a job or waiting for the PIRMI, RAI, pension, or they need to pay off loans.

The main social issues experienced by the beneficiaries are related to unemployment and housing costs. To face these difficulties, the interviewees rely on public support such as the bonus for energy poverty and for rent, unemployment benefits and free training courses. Owing to the fragmented nature of the wide range of aid measures provided, there is a risk of it losing effectiveness. The *Citizenship Pact for Inclusion 2016/2020* and the proposal for a citizenship income that can meet the real cost of living, are included both aim to address the effects of a piecemeal system of aid. In both cases, a structural approach to inequalities is found within a capability development framework.

In Athens, a different situation emerges, in which the normative approach to strengthen beneficieries' agency is compromised. On one hand, through a network of collaboration with the social and institutional fabric, aiming - in an emergency perspective - to satisfy basic needs; on the other hand, through a mechanism of passive food reception linked to food waste cycle.

In this way, the beneficiaries' autonomy and focus on his or her different goals and needs, are lacking, leading Kipoda to apply the principle of merely "compensating for shortcomings". Indeed, Kipoda and the strong local solidarity networks (municipalities, foundations and private individuals) that supports it, play a decisive role in meeting the basic needs of people who, due to the economic crisis and the lack of adequate integration of lost entitlements, are forced to depend on external help. As highlighted by Vathakou (2015), in order to cope with the effects of the economic recession and austerity measures, the State is trying to replace the public welfare system with a "pilot" social programmes based on close cooperation between local public authorities and collective initiatives.

The process of strengthening the agency of beneficiaries that Kipoda would like to promote, is hindered by four main obstacles:

- the absence of public financial support and a legislative framework that can stimulate the work of collective actions of solidarity and voluntary activities;
- The role of mere "intermediary" prevents Kipoda from having complete control and autonomy over its work.;
- Kipoda's downsized workforce cannot support beneficiaries in their job seeking;
- Kipoda and the public employment agency do not communicate and do not cooperate.

The prevailing nature of Kipoda's approach to compensate for shortcomings is also reflected in a weak capability to give voice, structured around awareness-raising projects to increase donations of basic goods by private companies and local public institutions. However, there is no advocacy effort to change the structural conditions of a state of poverty.

In addition, Kipoda's efforts in distributing donated food, compromise the nutritional needs of people who do not seem to have a sufficiently diversified diet. As a result, the social use of food is also affected: people change their eating patterns as well as having diminished opportunities for conviviality. The women interviewed are more vulnerable to the effects of receiving precooked meals passively. This seriously affects the sense of autonomy and control over one's own food self-sufficiency. Therefore, the prevailing mindset of merely meeting needs does not address the root causes of poverty, and also shapes the consequent adaptive choices of the beneficiaries, with clear repercussions on capabilities and human achievements.

Concluding Remarks 8

8.1 City-Based Initiatives Against Food Insecurity: From a Productivist to a *Capabilities-Oriented* Perspective

The economic crisis and the associated austerity measures have had a significant impact on the living conditions of Europe's citizens. Starting from national and European surveys on the rise in poverty and social exclusion, this book aims to look deeper into the problem of food insecurity, through an interpretative lens that can enable a holistic and systematic study.

In this regard, the capability approach is taken as a key theoretical framework. In anti-poverty programmes, the capability approach aims to achieve the transition "*from freedom from want towards freedom to act*" (Hemerijck, 2017, p. 12; 2018). In other words, these programmes aim to activate people and go beyond the mere meeting of basic needs. Activation is analysed in terms of empowerment, that is, in terms of expanding and strengthening a person's agency, acting and realising his or her life goals. Activation must inspire programmes to address poverty, by looking at the beneficiaries as *agents* and not as passive recipients of top-down policies.

Providing spaces for communication and reflection open to the participation of all, giving voice to people and understanding activation in terms of *freedom for all,* are the constituent aspects of the capability approach. These characteristics help throw light on the "transformative" nature of the capability approach in regard to socio-economic circumstances (Bonvin and Laruffa, 2018).

What has emerged from the empirical study, on which this book is based, is that -at national level- food insecurity is mostly tackled through broader anti-poverty programmes, for example, in the form of social cards for the payment of household and basic needs, or minimum income schemes. These might be social debit cards, that sometimes have spending limits or restrictions on the types of products that can be purchased.

D. Bernaschi, *Collective Actions of Solidarity against Food Insecurity*, RaumFragen: Stadt – Region – Landschaft, https://doi.org/10.1007/978-3-658-31375-3_8

This aspect implies a standpoint of analysis that considers people, who are experiencing poverty, as basically unreliable and also -to some extent- personally responsible for their own state of deprivation. As a result, a paternalistic vision emerges, taking the form of guidance and control which might somehow protect them from their self-damaging instincts.

In addition, there is a tendency to view the fight against food insecurity, by looking almost exclusively at the distribution of food resources, through the FEAD programme, food banks or church food parcels. The distribution of standardised products chosen by someone else, however, clashes with a vision of people as holders of different experiences and needs: cultural, social and nutritional ones. The main idea behind these aid programmes is that, it is sufficient to give the poor some ready-made food: the classic cardboard package containing pasta, cans of beans and long-life milk.

The result, therefore, is both a problematisation of poverty on a purely individual level, in which there is no focus on social conversion factors, and also a problematisation of food insecurity from a purely *productivist* perspective, with no regard for the social dimension of deprivation. Therefore, an approach is missing that looks at food insecurity in terms of lack of autonomy, control and freedom over one's own food security, with its consequences in terms of relational and convivial needs.

As a result, the role of some anti-poverty policies is hindered by their constrained access and limited voice which is actually instrumental in understanding the drivers of deprivation and the ways out of it. This failure explains, to some extent, the rise of several initiatives, at the local level, promoted by different social actors, in which the problem of food insecurity is addressed in a social and collective ways.

A social ferment that increasingly highlights the leading role of cities in offering innovative and participatory responses to global issues. Food and city is a dual notion that underlines the ways local dimensions contribute to a new definition of food security and the consequent contrasting policies.

The collective actions of solidarity, which are the focus of this book, are based on the increasingly active involvement of beneficiaries. This perspective has been strengthened by the use of qualitative research methods (e.g. interviews with coordinators and beneficiaries). Indeed, by "giving voice" to all social actors and, above all, to the beneficiaries of these initiatives, it is possible to reconstruct the life paths and identify the factors and events that have determined a decline or a strengthening of capabilities. By doing so, it is possible to steer the resulting anti-poverty policies.

The selection of research tools and the structure of the empirical study, are shaped to move away from a mere description of the social phenomena, that should be embraced in favour of an analysis aimed at:

- identifying the most affected social categories and the main drivers of food insecurity;
- identifying the influence played by the social and institutional context (in the form of rights, resources and legal channels to access them) on the generative process of individual capabilities;

- assessing the impact of collective actions of solidarity in terms of capabilities: are they able to strengthen the agency of their beneficiaries? Are they able, through a network of collaboration between other collective initiatives and the local public institutions, to strengthen the capability of voice for an effective social change?;
- highlighting a different problematisation of food insecurity, linking it to the issue of food waste and, therefore, to the inefficiencies of the production system, or to a dimension that is more linked to people's substantive freedoms.

The most vulnerable social categories are identified as: families with minors (Rome), single or divorced women aged over 55 with minors (Barcelona), unmarried people or divorced women with children (Athens).

The main drivers of food insecurity can be found in unemployment, low-paid, temporary and off-the-books jobs. In addition to these common data, there are differences at the local level. In Rome, the precipitating factors for a state of deprivation, are the difficulties faced by women in finding a job that allows them to meet their family commitments, and divorce as a relational failure. In Barcelona, it is the cost of living, while in Athens, the main social issues are debts with banks and the EFKA, and the dual "relational" and "economic" failure experienced in divorce.

The research has highlighted the role of the social context in influencing the generative process of capabilities, which occurs through social conversion factors (labour segregation for some social categories; high cost of housing; health system deficiencies, normative factors (absence or presence of public integration of lost entitlements[1]) and cultural ones (in terms of deep-rooted values and experiences of cooperation and solidarity), thus affecting the conversion of the initial endowments into substantive freedoms.

The social and institutional context also plays a decisive role in steering the practices of collective actions of solidarity, and their impact in terms of individual capabilities and social change. In contexts where basic needs are compromised, the initiatives shape their solidarity action according to their satisfaction, and the emergency approach takes the place of a more structured assessment of food insecurity in terms of autonomy and free access to food.

Moreover, a network of collaboration between collective actions of solidarity and local public institutions is crucial for strengthening beneficiaries' agency and the capability for voice, facilitating an actual change in the structural conditions underlying poverty. The absence of this synergy risks limiting the action of the initiatives, restricting their role to compensating for shortcomings or providing weak "capabilities oriented" actions.

[1]The inability to access unemployment benefit due to irregular employment status, and/or the high eligibility criteria for minimum income measures.

The study of anti-food insecurity initiatives has made it possible to identify a common thread which finds its deepest expression in the Greek word: *philoxenia*. *Xenia* refers to the value hospitality, "welcoming" and "caring for" those who are far from home. Regarding food security initiatives, the concept of "being far from home" seems to be more elaborate, as it refers to social solitude as a deprivation of substantive freedoms. Food conveys "*xenia*" to the extent of almost identifying with it; as a means of survival, food is also charged with relational, social, community and dignity value, through which to create human ties (Keane, 2003). In this way, an "individual" condition of social marginalisation turns into a sense of belonging to a community.

Collective actions of solidarity encompass an idea of social solidarity within socially responsible action, which strengthens the capability for giving voice, in order to foster the change in the root cause of poverty. Hence, their power is transformative, creative and future-oriented. While in Rome, there is the experience of Caritas with the Alliance against Poverty, and in Barcelona, the Citizenship Pact for Social Inclusion, in Athens the scenario is different. A social context weakened by the economic crisis and austerity measures, has shaped Kipoda's emergency approach. Regarding the Solidarity Kitchen, the capability for voice remains crystallised in a "weak" cooperative relationship with local public institutions, aimed only at increasing donations of basic goods.

A number of conclusions can be drawn from the initiatives assessed. Owing to the lack of collaboration with local public institutions and the presence of "free" access to food linked to "food waste", the Emporium can be defined as a "weak" *capabilities-oriented* initiative, but only for the selected target. Thanks to the strong synergy between the local public institutions and collective solidarity initiatives, as well as, the free access to market resources, the Solidarity Card can be defined as a "strong" *capabilities-oriented* initiative. Conversely, owing to a lack of freedom of food choice and the presence of collaborative networks structured around meeting basic needs, the Solidarity Kitchen is an initiative that is focused merely on *compensating for shortcomings*.

8.2 From "Food to Freedom" and From "Freedom to Food"

There are three aspects worth exploring for a reflection on social policies. First, this book highlights the importance of adopting a *capabilities-oriented* normative approach in the policy-making process. Such an approach not only focuses on the distributive dimension of resources, but also on the universal access criteria. The universality of access includes even those people who have no potential in terms of human capital, and is crucial because it can create a return in capabilities even from people experiencing severe deprivations (Appadurai, 2014). In doing so, the risk of exclusion and the onset of the Matthew effect are avoided.

Second, it has established that food insecurity, poverty and social exclusion, are dynamic and complex concepts, requiring close collaboration between and among any social actors, to enable shared action to tackled them. Therefore, what is needed is not only an active and creative social fabric but also the presence of democratic institutions (Sen, 1999), and a collaborative institutional arena that can capture and embrace the innovative stimuli coming from collective actions of solidarity (e.g. the Solidarity Card in Barcelona is inspired by the Italian Caritas' *Carta Equa* project).

Thus, the political context is crucial. A democratic and inclusive political strategy allows collective actions of solidarity to play a distinctive role in strengthening people's substantive freedoms. This book highlights the cooperative conflict dimension (Sen, 1990). In fact, collective actions of solidarity are conceived neither in romantic terms, with the public institutions charging them with "unexpected" social responsibility, nor as a "counter-power" to central power. On the contrary, they are seen as an arena of conflicting interests, which calls for a system of cooperation. Thus, the fostering of individual capabilities requires a cooperative and collaborative dimension; without it, the conflict prevails, condemning the collective actions of solidarity to be "niche" experiences with a compromised effects in terms of capabilities.

The third and last aspect pointed out in the book, concerns food insecurity. The first step to addressing it, even in developed countries, is to consider the social, nutritional and relational aspects of food, including food availability, access and food safety. It is important to look at the distribution of resources, but it is also important to pay attention to how these resources are effectively converted into substantive freedoms. This allows the social dimension of deprivation to be taken into account in terms of capabilities deprivation.

As a basic capability, food security is multidimensional, it relates to environmental sustainability as well as to the actual access to food. Therefore, it is crucial to address the need to move food production towards greater sustainability in "environmental" and "human" terms: food production for a growing world population, in a context of compromised natural resources, and respect for the environment, food producers and food quality. At the same time, it is necessary to broaden the analysis and consider all those conditions that deprive people of substantive freedoms and control over their use of food. The latter has a twofold significance: nutritional and socio-relational ones.

Thus, two key dimensions of food security can be highlighted:

- the sustainably and fairly food **production** and **consumption**;
- ensuring that all people have **access** to safe and nutritious food fairly and sustainably produced.

Food waste cannot be a structural solution to food security. Distributing the surpluses of production does not, in fact, necessarily alter the original inequalities. Consequently, on one hand, waste needs a targeted solution that can intervene at both production and consumption level. Food insecurity, on the other hand, requires a focus on the entitlements that ensure the access to food available on the market. It is crucial to adopt methods of production and distribution that can move away from an approach that is only aimed at buffering what has become a structural issue.

Indeed, linking food insecurity to food waste ties the analysis to the "quantity" of deprivation. In fact, connecting production system issues (e.g. excess production, unsold products because of packaging problems, and products nearly their expiry date) to one of food insecurity, removes the focus from the *social drivers* of deprivation which, as a result, do not actually be changed.

Moreover, the distribution of food to people in need, as an emergency measure, does not consider the social nature of deprivation: i.e. autonomy, freedoms and relationships that are socially compromised. Therefore, programmes which address food insecurity should not only focus on food distribution, namely on the need to "feed" people, but also on the need to foster the substantive freedoms (namely, *capabilities*), *agency* and the *capability for voice*. Consequently, in the context of policies aimed at strengthening capabilities, the dual idea of "food and freedom" should be the main paradigm, focusing on its interdependence: from "food to freedom", and from "freedom to food".

"'*Grub first, then ethics', thus runs a much quoted aphorism of Bertolt Brecht. There is undoubtedly some sense in this phased gradation. Ethics may seem like a much more remote and much less immediate subject than the command over food that we need to survive. Freedom too-as an important concept in ethics-may seem to be far less immediate than the compelling demands of grabbing grub. But this contrast is quite artificial.* ***The provision of food is indeed a central issue in general social ethics, since so much in human life does depend on the ability to find enough to eat.*** *(…)* ***On the other side, freedom may also causally influence the success of the pursuit of food for all*** *(…) Insofar as public policy to combat hunger and starvation—including rapid intervention against threatening famines—may depend on the existence and efficiency of political pressure groups to induce governments to act*" (Sen, 1987b, p. 2, emphasis added).

Appendix 1: Emporium of Solidarity in Rome

D. Bernaschi, *Collective Actions of Solidarity against Food Insecurity,* RaumFragen: Stadt – Region – Landschaft, https://doi.org/10.1007/978-3-658-31375-3

Appendix 2: The Solidarity Card in Barcelona

D. Bernaschi, *Collective Actions of Solidarity against Food Insecurity,* RaumFragen: Stadt – Region – Landschaft, https://doi.org/10.1007/978-3-658-31375-3

Appendix 3: The Solidarity Kitchen in Athens

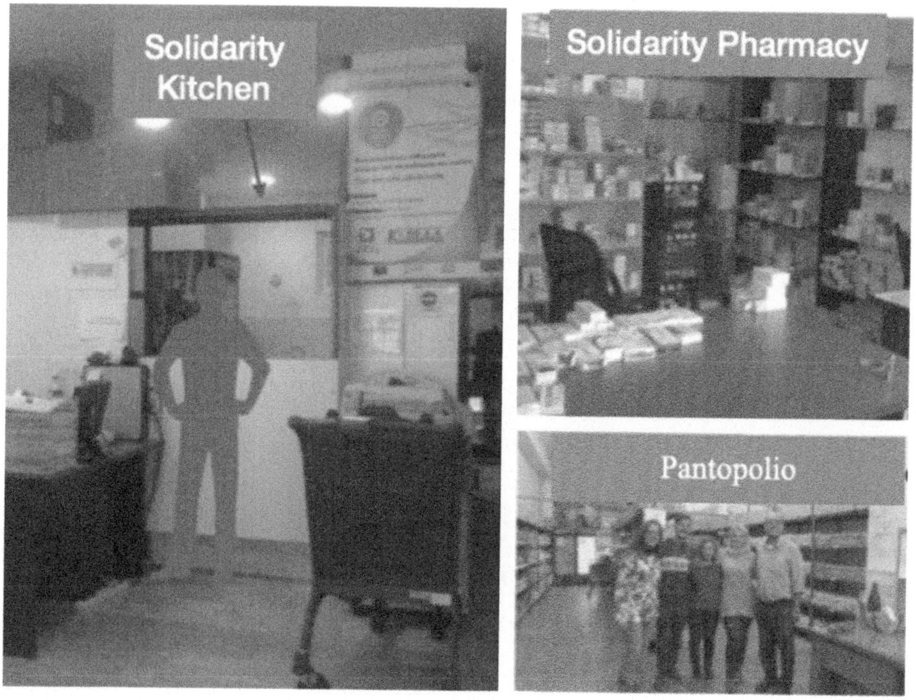

D. Bernaschi, *Collective Actions of Solidarity against Food Insecurity,* RaumFragen: Stadt – Region – Landschaft, https://doi.org/10.1007/978-3-658-31375-3

References

Alberich, T. 2016. *Desde las Asociaciones de Vecinos al 15M y las mareas ciudadanas: breve historia de los movimientos sociales.* Dykinson: http://digital.casalini.it/9788490856734.

Alkire, S. 2002. *Valuing Freedoms: Sen's Capability Approach and Poverty Reduction*, Oxford University Press.

Alkire, S. 2005. "Subjective quantitative studies of human agency". *Social Indicators Research*, No 74, pp. 217–260.

Alkire, S., Deneulin, S. 2009. "The Human Development and Capability Approach" in DENEULIN, S. and L. SHAHANI (eds) *An Introduction to Human Development and Capability Approach*, Chapter 2.

Appadurai, A. 2014. *Il futuro come fatto culturale*, Milan, Italy, La Feltrinelli.

Arampatzi, A. 2017. "Contentious spatialities in an era of austerity: Everyday politics and 'struggle communities' in Athens, Greece". *Political Geography*. 60. 47–56. https://doi.org/10.1016/j.polgeo.2017.03.010.

Atkinson, A.B. and Bourguignon, F. 2000. "Introduction: Income distribution and economics". *Handbook of income distribution*, 1, pp. 1–58.

Ballet, J., Dubois, J.-L., Mahieu, F.-R. 2007. "Responsibility for each other's freedom: agency as the source of collective capability". *J. Hum. Dev.* 8, 185–201.

Bagnasco, A., Piselli, F., Pizzorno, A., Trigilia, C. 2001. *Il capitale sociale: istruzioni per l'uso*. Il Mulino.

Bauman, Z. 2005. *Globalizzazione e Glocalizzazione*. Saggi scelti a cura di Peter Beilharz.

BCFN, MUFPP. 2018. *Food and Cities. Il ruolo delle città nel raggiungimento degli Obiettivi di Sviluppo Sostenibile,* Barilla Center for Food and Nutritions.

Beck, U. 1992. *Risk Society: Towards a New Modernity*. SAGE.

Beck, U. 2003. *La società cosmopolita. Prospettive dell'epoca postnazionale*. Bologna, Italy, Il Mulino.

Beckert, J. 2010. "How Do Fields Change? The Interrelations of Institutions, Networks, and Cognition in the Dynamics of Markets", *Organization Studies* 31:605–627.

Bentham, J. 1823. *An Introduction to the Principles of Morals and Legislation*. W. Pickering.

Blanco, I., Cruz, H. 2014. "Crisis, urban segregation and social innovation in Catalonia", *ECPR General Conference* Glasgow 3–6 September 2014, Panel P232: Alternative forms of Resilience in Times of Crisis.

Bifulco, L., and Mozzana, C. 2011. "La dimensione sociale delle capacità: fattori di conversione, istituzioni e azione pubblica". *RASSEGNA ITALIANA DI SOCIOLOGIA*.

Bonvin, J.-M., Thelen, T. 2003. "Deliberative Democracy and Capabilities. The impact and significant of capability for voice". *Conferenza sul Capability Approach*, 7–9 settembre, Università di Pavia.

Bonvin, J.-M., Farvaque, N. 2005. "What Informational Basis for Assessing Job-Seekers? Capabilities vs. Preferences". *Review of Social Economy*, 63 (2), 269–290.

D. Bernaschi, *Collective Actions of Solidarity against Food Insecurity,* RaumFragen: Stadt – Region – Landschaft, https://doi.org/10.1007/978-3-658-31375-3

Bonvin, J.-M., Farvaque, N. 2007. "A Capability Approach to individualised and tailor-made activation", in Van Berkel, R. E Valkenbutg, B. (eds), *Making it personal. Individualising activation services in the EU*, p 45–66, The Policy Press.

Bonvin, J.-M. 2012. "Individual working lives and collective action. An introduction to capability for work and capability for voice". *Transfer: European Review of Labour and Research*, 18 (1), 9–18.

Bonvin, J.-M., and Rosenstein, E. 2015. "Contractualising social policies: A way towards more active social citizenship and enhanced capabilities?" In R. Ervik, N. Kildal and E. Nilssen (Eds.), *New Contractualism in European Welfare Policies* (p. 47–72). Aldershot: Ashgate.

Bonvin, J.-M-, and Laruffa, F. 2018. "Beyond Social Investment, The Contribution of the Capability Approach for Theorizing Welfare Reform", *Conference Paper, ESPAnet Italia*, 13–15 Settembre 2018, Firenze.

Bosi, L., Zamponi, L. 2015. "Direct Social Actions and Economic Crises: The relationship between forms of action and socio-economic context in Italy", *PACO*, Issue 8(2) 2015: 367–391. https://doi.org/10.1285/i20356609v8i2p367.

Bourdieu, P. 1979. *La distinzione: Critica sociale del gusto*, Bologna, Italy, Il Mulino.

Bourdieu P., 1985. "The forms of capital", in *Handbook of theory and research for the sociology of education*, J.G. Richardson, 1985, Westport: Greenwood.

Campiglio L., Rovati G. 2009. *La povertà alimentare in Italia: prima indagine quantitativa e qualitativa*. Milan, Italy, Guerini e associati.

Calbò, I., Sanahuja, R., Thibos, C. 2016. "Barcellona: City of Refuge". *Open Democracy*, 26 Settembre. http://www.opendemocracy.net/mediterranean-joutneys-in-hope/cameron-thibos-ignasi-calb-ram-n-sanahuja/barcelona-city-of-refuge.

Calhoun, C. J. 1998. "The public good as social and cultural project", In: W.W. Powell, E.S. Clemens. 1998. *Private Action and Public Good*, Yale University Press.

Calhoun, C. J. 2002. "Imagining solidarity: Cosmopolitanism, constitutional patriotism, and the public sphere". *Public culture*, *14*(1), 147–171.

Chiappero-Martinetti, E. and Venkatapuram, S. 2014. "The Capability Approach: A Framework for Population Studies", *African Population Studies* Vol 28, No. 2 June 2014.

Cleaver, F. 1999. "Paradoxes of participation: questioning participatory approaches to development", *Journal of International Development*, 11(4), pp. 597–612.

Coleman-Jensen A.J., Nord M., Andrews M., Carlson S. 2012. *Household Food Security in the United States in 2011*, Economic Research Report Number 141.

Comin, F. 2001. "Operationalizing Sen's Capability Approach", Paper prepared for the *Conference Justice and Poverty: examining Sen's Capability Approach*, Cambridge 5–7 June 2001.

Comim, F., 2008. *Measuring capabilities. The capability approach: concepts, measures and application*. Cambridge UP, Cambridge, pp. 157–200.

Crane, A. 2000. Corporate greening as amoralization. *Organization Studies*, 21(4), 673–696.

Crespi, F., Moscovici, S. 2001. *Solidarietà in questione. Contributi teorici e analisi empiriche*, Milan, Italy, Booklet.

Crespi, F. 2013. *Esistenza-come-realtà. Contro il predominio dell'economia*. Salerno, Italy, Orthotes.

Cristancho, C., Loukakis, A. 2018. "A Comparative Regional Perspective on Alternative Action Organization Responses to the Economic Crisis Across Europe", *American Behavioral Scientist*, Aprile 2018.

Crow, G. 2002. *Social solidarities: Theories, identities and social change*. Open University Press.

Cruz, H., Martinez, R., Ismael, B. 2017. "Crisis, Urban segregation and social innovation in Catalonia," Partecipazione e Conflitto, xx(x) Special issue: *Alternative Forms of Re-silience Confronting Hard Economic Times: A South European Perspective: xx.*

CSVnet. 2015. "La carica degli empori solidali. Dai Centri di Servizio per il Volontariato proposte concrete per la lotta allo spreco e il contrasto alle nuove povertà". Available at: http://www.csvnet.it/press/siparladinoi/comunicati-stampa/1710-la-carica-.

D'Alisa, G., Forno, F., Maurano, S. 2015. "Mapping the redundancy of collective actions", *PACO*, Issue 8(2) 2015: 328–342 https://doi.org/10.1285/i20356609v8i2p328.

Dahrendorf, R. 1989. *Il conflitto sociale nella modernità. Saggio sulla politica della libertà*, Rome, Italy, Laterza.

Dahrendorf, R. 1993. *Per un nuovo liberalismo,* Rome, Italy, Laterza.

Dahrendorf, R. 1996. "Economic Opportunity, Civil Society and Political Liberty". In *Development and Change,* Volume 27, Issue 2, April 1996, Pages 229–249. International Institute of Social Studies, The Hague.

Dahrendorf, R. 2006. *Quadrare il cerchio. Benessere economico, coesione sociale e libertà politic*a, Rome, Italy, Laterza.

Dahrendorf, R. 2009. *Quadrare il cerchio. Ieri e Oggi.* Rome, Italy, Laterza.

Das Gupta, M., Grandvoinnet, H., Romani, M. 2000. "State-synergies in development: laying the basis for collective action", *Policy Research Working Paper 2439*, World Bank, Washington, D.C.

Davis, O., Baumberg, G.B. 2016. "Did Food Insecurity rise across Europe after the 2008 Crisis? An analysis across welfare regimes". *Social Policy and Society*, ISSN 1474-7464.

Dean, H. 2009. "Critiquing capabilities: The distractions of a beguiling concept". *Critical Social Policy*, Vol 29, Issue 2, pp. 261–278.

Deneulin, S. 2008. "Beyond Individual Freedom and Agency: Structures of Living Together in Sen's Capability Approach to Development". In S. Alkire, F. Comim, and M. Qizilbash (Eds.), *The Capability Approach: Concepts, Measures and Application (*pp. 105–124). Cambridge: Cambridge University Press. https://doi.org/10.1017/cbo9780511492587.

Deneulin, S., McGregor, J. A., 2009. "The Capability Approach and the Politics of a Social Conception of Wellbeing". Working Paper. Bath: *Wellbeing in Developing Countries*/University of Bath. (Wellbeing in Developing Countries (WeD) Working Papers; WeD Working Paper 09).

Deneulin, S., Shahani, L. 2009. *An Introduction to the Human Development and Capability Approach.* Earthscan in the UK and US.

De Filippo, E., De Stefano, D., Dolente, F., Oliviero, L., Pisacane, L., Pugliese, E. 2012. *DIRITTI VIOLATI.* Dedalus.

De Munck, J. 2008. "Qu'est-ce qu'une capacité?". In Jean de Munck and Bénédicte Zimmermann (dir.): *La liberté au prisme des capacités.* Paris, Éditions de l'École des Hautes Études en Sciences Sociales.

De Muro P., Monni S, and Tridico P. 2011. "Knowledge-based economy and social exclusion: shadow and light in the Roman socioeconomic model". *INTERNATIONAL JOURNAL OF URBAN AND REGIONAL RESEARCH*, Vol. 35(6), 1212–1238.

Dietz, W.H. 1995. "Does Hunger Cause Obesity?". Pediatrics, May 1995, Volume 95/ISSUE 5.

Dick, M, Suseela, R., Di Gregorio, M., McCarthy, N. 2004. "Methods for studying collective action in rural development:," CAPRi working papers 33, International Food Policy Research Institute (IFPRI).

Dongier, P., Van Domelen,J., Ostrom, E., Ryan, A., Wakeman, W., Bebbington, A., Alkire, S., Esmail, T., Polski, M. 2004. "Community-Driven Development", Volume 1 – Core Techniques and Cross-Cutting Issues.

Dowler, E. 2002. "Food and Poverty in Britain: Rights and Responsibilities". Social Policy Administration, Volume 36, Issue 6, December 2002, pp. 698–717.

Dowler. E.A., Kneafsey, M., Lambie, H., Inman, A., Collier, R. 2011. "Thinking about 'food security': engaging with UK consumers". Crit.Pub. Health, 21(4), pp. 403–416.

Dowler, E., Lambie-Mumford, H. 2015. "Introduction: Hunger, Food and Social Policy in Austerity". Social Policy and Society, Vol. 14, No. 3, pp. 411–415.

Dreze, J., Sen, A.K. 1989. *Hunger and Public Action*. Oxford, UK: Oxford University Press.

Dreze, J., Sen, A.K. 2002. *India, Development and Participation*. Oxford, UK: Oxford University Press.

Dueilla, M. and Turrini, A. 2014. "Poverty developments in the EU after the crisis: a look a main driver", ECFINM Economic Brief, Issue 31.

Duncan, J. 2015. "Greening global food governance", *Canadian Food Studies/La Revue canadienne des études sur l'alimentation*, 2(2), 335–344.

Eder, K. 2015. "Afterword: The Crisis of Europe: A Case of Creative Destruction—Descandalizing the Crisis of Europe as an Experimental Case of Social Evolution". In *Europe's Prolonged Crisis* (pp. 270–289). Palgrave Macmillan, London.

Elias, N. 1988. *Il processo di civilizzazione*. Bologna, Italy, Il Mulino.

European Commission. 2010. *Preparatory Study on Food Waste Across EU 27*. Bruxelles.

European Commission. 2015. *The Fund for European Aid to the Most Deprived (FEAD) Breaking the vicious circle of poverty and deprivation*. Bruxelles.

Eurostat. 2019. "People at risk of poverty or social exclusion". Available at: https://ec.europa.eu/eurostat/statistics-explained/index.php/People_at_risk_of_poverty_or_social_exclusion#Number_of_people_at_risk_of_poverty_or_social_exclusion.

Evans, P. 2002. "Collective Capabilities, Culture, and Amartya Sen's Development as Freedom". *Studies in Comparative International Development*, 37:2, pp. 54–60.

Fioramonti, L., Kononykhina, O. 2014. "Measuring the Enabling Environment of Civil Society: A Global Capability Index" (Ferbuary 3, 2014). https://ssrn.com/abstract=2518325 or https://doi.org/10.2139/ssrn.2518325.

FAO-Food and Agriculture Organization. 1996. *Rome Declaration on World Food Security and World Food Summit Plan of Action. Proceedings of World Summit on Food Security,* FAO. Rome, Italy.

FAO-Food and Agriculture Organization. 2013. *The Food Insecurity Experience Scale Development of a Global Standard for Monitoring Hunger Worldwide,* FAO, Rome, Italy.

Frazer, H., and Marlier, E. 2016. "Minimum Income Schemes in Europe. A study of national policies", *European Social Policy Network* (ESPN), Bruxelles, European Commission.

Frigo, A. 2015. "Il Fead", In: *Dopo la crisi. Costruire il Welfare*. Rapporto 2015, Caritas Italiana.

Fukuda-Parr, S. 2003. "The Human Development Paradigma: operationalizing Sen's Ideas on Capabilities". *Feminist Economics* 9(2–3), 2003, 301–317.

Gascon, J., Montagut, X. 2015. *Banco de alimentos : ¿combatir el hambre con las sobras?*. Barcellona, Spain, Icaria Editorial SA.

Giddens, A. 1990. *The Consequences of Modernity*. Stanford, CA: Stanford University Press.

Gramaglia, E., Bolzoni, M. 2016. *Il reddito di base*. Rome, Italy, Ediesse.

Granovetter, M.1997. *La forza dei legami deboli e altri saggi*, trad.it. Napoli, Liguori.

Guidi, R., Andretta, M. 2015. "Between resistance and resilience. How do Italian solidarity purchase groups change in times of crisis and austerity?" *Partecipazione e Conflitto*, 8(2), 443–477.

Hanfstaengl, E. M. 2010. *Impact of the global economic crises on civil society organizations*. UN.

Haq, M. U. 1996. *Reflections on Human Development*, Oxford University Press, Oxford, UK.

Hemerijck, A. 2017. *The Uses of Social Investment*. Oxford, Oxford University Press, pp. 379–412.

Hemerijck, A. 2018. "Social investment as a policy paradigm", *Journal of European Public Policy,* 25:6, 810–827.

Hirschman, A. 2002. *Lealtà defezione protesta,* Bompiani, Roma.

Holt Giménez, E., and Shattuck, A. 2011. "Food crises, food regimes and food movements: rumblings of reform or tides of transformation?", *The Journal of peasant studies*, 38(1), 109–144.

Huliaras, A. 2015. "Greek Civil Society: The Neglected Causes of Weakness" In: Jenny Clarke, Asteris Huliaras and Dimitri A. Sotiropoulos, eds., *Austerity and the Third Sector in Greece: Civil Society at the European Frontline*, Farnham, Surrey: Ashgate, p. 9–27.

Ibrahim, S. 2006. "From individual to collective capabilities: The Capability Approach as a Conceptual Framework for Self-help". *Journal of Human Development and Capabilities*, 7(3), pp. 397–416.

Ibrahim, S. 2013. "Collective capabilities: what are they and why are they important?". *Collectivity in the Capability Approach. E-Bulletin of the Human Development and Capability Association*, No 22, June 2013, pp. 4–8.

Ibrahim, S. 2017. "How to Build Collective Capabilities: The 3C-Model for Grassroots-Led Development". *Journal of Human Development and Capabilities*, Vol. 18, 2017, 197–22 pp.

Ibrahim, S., Alkire, S. 2007. "Agency and Empowerment: A Proposal for Internationally Comparable Indicators". *Oxford Development Studies*,35:4, pp. 379–403.

Ibrahim, S., Hulme, D. 2010. "Has Civil Society Helped the Poor? A Review of the Roles and Contributions of Civil Society to Poverty Reduction" (April 16, 2010). Available at SSRN: https://ssrn.com/abstract=1590909.

Illich, I. 1972. *Tools for conviviality*. New York, USA: Harper and Row.

ILO. 1999. *Decent Work,* International Labour Conference, 87th Session, Geneva.

Isin, E.F. 2009. *Citizenship in flux: the figure of the activist citizen*, Palgrave Macmillan, Issue 29, 367–388.

Kantzara, V. 2014. "Solidarity in times of Crisis: emergent Practices and Potential for Paradigmatic Change. Notes from greece". *Studi di Sociologia*, 261–280.

Keane, J. 2003. *Global Civil Society?*, Cambridge University Press.

Krishna, A., Uphoff, N., Esman, M. 1997. *Reason for hope: instructive experiences in rural development*, Kumarian Press, Connecticut.

Kousis, M., M. Giugni and C. Lahusen. 2016. "Action Organization Analysis: A New, online-based Approach extending Protest Event Analysis through Hubs-based website Analysis", paper to be presented in the *ECPR General Conference Panel, Transnational Solidarity and Alternative Action Organizations in European Countries at Times of Crisis,* Open Section, Prague Sept.7–10 2016.

Kousis, M., Paschou, M. 2017. "Alternative Forms of resilience, A typology of approaches for the study of Citizen Collective Responses in Hard Economic Times", *PACO*, Issue 10(1) 2017: 136–168.

Kousis, M. 2017. "Alternative Forms of Resilience confronting Hard Times: A South European Perspective", *PACO*, Issue 10(1) 2017: 119–135 https://doi.org/10.1285/i20356609v10i1p119.

Lahusen, C., Loukakis, A. 2016. "Spatial patterns of Alternative Action Organizations in Europe: building resilience in times of crisis where it is needed?",*10th ECPR General Conference Charles University in Prague* 7–10 September 2016.

Lambie-Mumford, H., Crossley, D., Jensen, E., Verbeke, M. and Dowler, E. 2014. *Household Food Security in the UK: A Review of Food Aid. Final Report*, University of Warwick and the Food Ethics Council, Warwick, UK.

Lambie-Mumford, H. and Dowler, E. 2014. "Rising use of "food aid" in the United Kingdom". *British Food Journal*, 116(9), pp. 1418–1425.

Lang, T., Barling, D. 2012. "Food security and food sustainability: reformulating the debate", *The Geographical Journal,* Volume 178, Issue 4.

Lash, S. 1993. "Reflexive Modernization: the aesthetic dimension". *Theory, Culture and Society*, 10(1), 1993, pp. 1–23.

Leonardi, L. 2001. *La dimensione sociale della globalizzazione*, Carocci.

Leonardi, L. 2009. "Capacitazioni, lavoro e welfare. La ricerca di nuovi equilibri tra stato e mercato: ripartire dall'Europa?", *Stato e mercato,* No. 85 (1) (aprile 2009), pp. 31–61.

Leonardi, L. 2018. "La crisi dell'Europa. La 'distruzione creativa' e le nuove solidarietà sociali", CSE *Working Papers* 18, 2 Marzo 2018.

Levi-Strauss, C.1966. *Il crudo e il cotto*, Il Saggiatore, Milan, Italy.

LIVEWHAT. 2016. *Living with Hard Times. How Citizens React to Economic Crises and Their Social and Political Consequences,*https://www.unige.ch/livewhat/wp-content/uploads/2014/07/Deliverable-6.1.pdf.

Loopstra, R., Reeves, A., Taylor-Robinson, D., Barr, B., McKee, M., Stuckler, D. 2015. "Austerity, sanctions, and the rise of food banks in the UK". *BMJ* (Clinical research ed), 350. h1775.

Lyberaki A. Tinios, P. 2014. "The Informal welfare State and the family: Invisible actors in the Greek drama", *Political Studies Review*, 2014 VOL 12, 193–208.

Maino F., Lodi Rizzini, C., Bandera, L. 2015, *Povertà alimentare in Italia: le risposte del secondo welfare*, Il Mulino.

Mann, A. 2019. *Voice and Participation in Global Food Politics.* London, UK, Routledge.

Mannheim, K. 1968. *Libertà, potere e pianificazione democratica.* Rome, Italy, Armando ed.

Marsden, T., Sonnino, R. 2008. "Rural Development and regional state. Denying multifunctional agriculture in the UK", *Journal of Rural Studies,* (24), pp. 422–431.

Marsden, T., Sonnino, R. 2012. "Human health and wellbeing and the sustainability of urban-regional food systems". *Curr. Opin. Environ. Sustain.* 4 (4), pp. 427–430.

Marsden, T. 2013. "From post-productionism to reflexive governance: Contested transitions in securing more sustainable food futures", *Journal of Rural Studies,* Volume 29, January 2013, Pages 123–134 Food Security.

Marques-Vidal, P., Waeber, G., Vollenweider, P., Bochud, M., Stringhini, S,Guessous, I. 2015. "Sociodemographic and Behavioural Determinants of a Healthy Diet in Switzerland". *Ann Nutr Metab.* 2015;67(2):87–95. https://doi.org/10.1159/000437393. Epub 2015 Sep 5.

Marx, K. 1875. *Critica al Programma di Gotha.* Edizioni in lingua estera, Mosca, 1947.

Matsaganis, M. 2011. "The welfare state and the crisis: the case of Greece". *Journal of European Social Policy*, 21(5), 501–512.

Matsaganis, M., e Leventi, C. 2014. "The Distributional Impact of Austerity and the Recession in Southern Europe", *South European Society and Politics,* 19:3, 393–412.

Matsaganis, M. 2014. "The crisis, the austerity, and social policy in Greece", *Social Policies*, 1(1), 65–76.

Matsaganis, M. 2017. "The contorted politics of guaranteed minimum income in Greece". *Working Paper,* Politecnico di Milano, Milan, Italy.

Mendes, W., and Sonnino, R. 2018. "Urban food governance in the Global North", *Handbook of Nature*, Sage London.

Mouzelis, N. 1995. "Greece in the twenty-first century: institutions and political culture". *Greece prepares for the twenty-first century*, 17–34.

Narayan, D., Chambers, R., Shah, M.K., Patti, P. 2000. *Voices of the Poor: Crying Out for Change.* The World Bank and Oxford University Press.

Narayan, D. 2005. *Measuring Empowerment: Cross-Disciplinary Perspectives.* Washington, D.C.: The World Bank.

Natili, M., Matsaganis, M., Jessoula, M. 2016. "Alla prova della crisi. Povertà e reddito minimo nell'Europa del Sud e dell'Est". *Working Paper-LPF*, No.5., Centro Einaudi.

Nussbaum, M. C. 1988. "The Good as Discipline, the Good as Freedom". In: Crocker, D. and T. Linden (eds.): *Ethics of Consumption: The Good Life, Justice, and Global Stewardship*, 312–341.

Nussbaum, M. C. 2000, *Women and Human Development: The Capabilities Approach*, Cambridge University Press.

Nussbaum, M.C. 2003. "Capabilities as fundamental entitlements: Sen and Social Justice", *Feminist Economics* 9(2–3), 2003, pp. 33–59.

Nussbaum, M. 2006. *Frontiers of Justice: Disability, Nationality, Species Membership*. Cambridge, MA: Harvard University Press.

Osmani, S. 1995. "The entitlement approach to famine: an assessment", in: K. Basu, P. Pattanaik and K. Suzumura (Eds) *Choice, Welfare and Development* (Oxford; Oxford University Press).

Ostrom, E. 1990. *Governing the commons: the evolution of institutions for collective action*, Cambridge University Press, Cambridge.

Papadaki, M., Kalogeraki, S. 2018. "Exploring Social and Solidarity Economy (SSE) during the Greek crisis", *Partecipazione e conflitto*, 11(1) 2018:38–69.

Pautz H., Komninou, M. 2013. "Reacting to 'Austerity Politics': The Tactic of Collective Expropriation in Greece", *Social Movement Studies*, 12(1): 103–110.

Pelenc, J., Bazile, D., Ceruti, C. 2015. "Collective capability and collective agency for sustainability: A case study", *Ecological Economics* 118:226–239. https://doi.org/10.1016/j.ecolecon.2015.07.001.

Perez e Matsaganis, M. (2018). "The Political Economy of Austerity in Southern Europe", *JournalNew Political Economy*, Volume 23, 2018.

Petropoulou C. 2013. "'Alternative Networks of Collectivities' and 'Solidarity-Cooperative Economy' in Greek cities: exploring their theoretical origins", *Journal of Regional Socio-economic* Issues, 3(2): 61–86.

Pulcini, E. 2009. *La cura del mondo. Paura e responsabilità nell'età globale*. Turin, Italy, Bollati Boringhieri.

Putnam, R. 1995. "Bowling Alone: America's Declining Social Capital", *Journal of Democracy*, January: pp. 65–78.

Putnam, R. D. 2000. Bowling alone: America's declining social capital. In *Culture and politics* (pp. 223–234). New York, Palgrave Macmillan.

Putnam, R. 2004. *Democracies in flux: The evolution of social capital in contemporary society*. Oxford University Press, USA.

Rao, V., Walton, M. 2004. *Culture and Public Action*, Stanford University Press, Palo Alto, California, pp 59–84.

Ranis, G., Stewart, F., Ramirez, A. 2000. "Economic Growth and Human Development". *World Development*, 2000, vol. 28, issue 2, 197–219.

Rakopoulos, T. 2014. "Resonance of Solidarity: Meanings of a Local Concept in Anti-austerity Greece", Journal of Modern Greek Studies, Volume 32, Number 2, October 2014, pp. 313–337, The Johns Hopkins University Press.

Rakopoulos, T. 2016. "Solidarity: the egalitarian tensions of a bridge-concept, Social Anthropology" (2016)24, 2 142–151, European Association of Social Anthropologists. https://doi.org/10.1111/1469-8676.1229.

Rauschmayer, F., Bauler, T., Schäpke, N. 2015. "Towards a thick understanding of sustainability transitions—linking transition management, capabilities and social practices", *Ecol. Econ.* 109, 211–221.

Rawls, J. 1971. *A Theory of Justice*. Harvard University Press.

Reinach, A. 1983. *The apriori foundations of civil law*. Aletheia 3: 1–142.

Robeyns, I. 2000. "An unworkable idea or a promising alternative? Sen's capability approach re-examined". *Center for Economic Studies, Discussions Paper Series (DPS)* 00.30 http://www.econ.kuleuven.be/ces/discussionpapers/default.htm.

Robeyns, I., 2003. "Sen's capability approach and gender inequality: selecting relevant capabilities". *Feminist economics*, 9(2–3), pp. 61–92.

Robeyns, I. 2005. "The Capability Approach: a theoretical survey", *Journal of Human Development,* Vol. 6, No. 1, March 2005.

Salais, R. 2003. "Social Exclusion and Capability". In: *Marginalisation and Social Exclusion,* May 2003, Alesund, Norway. <halshs-00430491>.

Salais, R. 2009. "Deliberative democracy and its informational basis: what lessons from the Capability Approach". *SASE (Society for the Advancement of Socio-Economics) Conference,* luglio 2009, Paris, France.

Salamon, L.M. 1994. "The Rise of the Nonprofit Sector". *Foreign Affairs*, Vol. 73, No. 4 (Jul.–Aug., 1994), pp. 109–122.

Sassen, S. 2003. *Le città nell'economia globale*, Bologna, Italy, Il Mulino.

Sassen, S. 2016. "The Global City: Enabling Economic Intermediation and Bearing Its Costs", *City and Community*, Volume15, Issue2, June 2016, p. 97–108, American Sociological Association.

Sandbu. 2015. *Europe's Orphan.The Future of the Euro and the Politics of Debt.* Princeton Press, USA.

Seyfang, G., Haxeltine, A. 2012. "Growing Grassroots Innovations: Exploring the Role of Community-Based Initiatives in Governing Sustainable Energy Transitions", *Environment and Planning C: Politics and Space*, Vol 30, Issue 3, pp. 381–400.

Sen, A. K. 1977. "Rational fools: A critique of the behavioral foundations of economic theory". *Philosophy and Public Affairs*, 317–344.

Sen, A. K. 1981. P*overty and famines: an essay on entitlement and deprivation*. Oxford, UK: Clarendon Press.

Sen, A.K. 1984. *Resources, Values and Development.* Oxford, UK: Basil Blackwell.

Sen, A.K. 1985. *Commodities and Capabilities*. Oxford India Paperbacks.

Sen, A.K. 1987a. "The Standard of Living", The Tanner Lectures, Cambridge: Cambridge University Press.

Sen, A. K. 1987b. "Food and freedom". In: Sutton, F.X. 1987. *A World to Make: Development in Perspective*. Transaction Publishers.

Sen A. K. 1990. "Gender and Cooperative Conflicts". In: Tinker, I. 1990. *Persistent Inequalities.* New York: Oxford University Press.

Sen, A.K. 1992a. *Inequality Reexamined*, Oxford, Oxford University Press.

Sen, A.K. 1992b. *Risorse, Valori e Sviluppo*. Turin, Italy, Bollati Boringhieri.

Sen, A.K. 1992c. Missing women, *BMJ: British Medical Journal, 304*(6827), 587.

Sen, A.K. 1997. *La libertà individuale come impegno sociale*. Bari-Rome, Italy: Laterza Edizioni.

Sen, A.K. 1999. *Development as Freedom*. Oxford, UK: Oxford UP.

Sen, A.K. 2000. "Social exclusion: concept, application, and scrutiny". *Social Development Papers No. 1*. Office of Environment and Social Development Asian Development Bank.

Sen, A.K. 2002. 'Symposium on Development as Freedom: Response to Commentaries', *Studies in Comparative International Development* 37(2): 78–86.

Sen, A.K. 2003. *Globalizzazione e Libertà*, Milan, Italy, Mondadori.

Sen, A.K. 2004. "Elements of a Theory of Human Rights", Volume 32, Issue 4, October 2004, p. 315–356.

Sen, A.K. 2009. *The Idea of Justice*, Harvard University Press.

Sen, A. 2012. "The snakes and ladders of Europe, The economic system we need", 10 Maggio 2012, Università Bocconi, Milan, Italy.

Schwan, G. 2017. "Cities to the rescue", *Green European Journal*, 30 Nov. 2017, https://www.greeneuropeanjournal.eu/cities-to-the-rescue/.

Scott, N.-R. 2007. "BOOK REVIEW Human Security: Reflections on Globalization and Intervention By Mary Kaldor", *Journal of Peace, Conflict and Development*, www.peacestudiesjournal.org.uk, Issue 15, March 2010.

Shahin J., Woodward A., Terzis G. 2013. *The impact of the crisis on civil society organisations in the EU: risks and opportunities*, Brussels: European Economic and Social Committee (available at http://ec.europa.eu/citizenship/pdf/eesc_qe-32-12-548-en-c_en.pdf).

Simiti, M. 2015. "Rage and Protest: The Case of the Greek Indiginant Movement". *Contention,* 3(2), 33–50.

Simiti, M. 2017. "Civil Society and the Economy: Greek Civil Society During the Economic Crisis", *Journal of Civil Society,* Vol. 13, Iss. 4, 2017.

Smith, A. 1759. *The Theory of Moral Sentiments.* Printed for Andrew Millar, in the Strand; and Alexander Kincaid and J. Bell, in Edinburgh.

Sonnino, R. 2016. "The new geography of food security: exploring the potential of urban food strategies". *The Geographical Journal,* Vol. 182, No. 2, pp. 190–200.

Sonnino, R. 2018. "Come le università e gli istituti di ricerca possono sostenere il pensiero progettuale nella definizione delle politiche alimentari", in BCFN, MUFPP. 2018. *Food and Cities. Il ruolo delle città nel raggiungimento degli Obiettivi di Sviluppo Sostenibile.*

Sotiropoulos, D.A., 2014. *Civil society in Greece in the wake of the economic crisis,* Konrad-Adenauer-Stiftung (KAS), Atene.

Sotiropoulos, D. A., Bourikos, D. 2014. "Economic crisis, social solidarity and the voluntary sector in Greece". *Journal of Power, Politics and Governance,* 2(2), 33–53.

Srinivasan, T.N., 1994. "Human development: a new paradigm or reinvention of the wheel?", *The American Economic Review*, 84(2), pp. 238–243.

Stewart, F. and Deneulin, S. 2002, "Amartya Sen's contribution to development thinking", *Studies in Comparative International Development*, 37(61), 61–70.

Stewart, F. 2005. "Groups and capabilities", *Journal of Human Development*, 6(2), pp. 185–204.

Stiglitz, J., Sen, A. K., and Fitoussi, J. P. 2009. *The measurement of economic performance and social progress revisited: reflections and overview.*

Thorp, R., Stewart, F., Heyer, A. 2003. "When and How Far is Group Formation a Route out of Chronic Poverty?", *conference Staying Poor: Chronic Poverty and Development Policy*, University of Manchester, 7–9 April 2003 (www.chronicpoverty.org).

Tilly, C. 1975. *The Formation of National States in Western Europe*, Princeton, Princeton University Press.

Tomassi, F., Lelo, K., Monni, S. 2016. "Roma, tra centro e periferie: come incidono le dinamiche urbanistiche sulle disuguaglianze socio-economiche". *28th Annual Congress of the Italian Society of Public Economics* (SIEP 2016), 22–23 Settembre 2016, Lecce, Italy.

UNDP. 1990. *Human Development Report,* Oxford University Press.

UNICEF. 2017. *Costruire il futuro -I bambini e gli Obiettivi di Sviluppo Sostenibile nei paesi ricchi-,* Report Card.

Varoufakis 2011. *The Global Minotaur: America, The True Origins of the Financial Crisis and the Future of the World Economy.* Zed Books.

Vathakou E. 2015. "Citizens' Solidarity Initiatives in Greece during the financial crisis" In: J. Clarke, A. Huliaras, D. Sotiropoulos (eds.), *Austerity and the Third Sector in Greece: Civil Society at the European Frontline*, London: Ashgate (pp. 167–192).

Von Jacobi, N., Ziegler, R., Edmiston, D. 2015. "Tackling Marginalisation through Social Innovation? Examining the EU Social Innovation Policy Agenda from a Capabilities Perspective", January 2017, *Journal of Human Development and Capabilities* 18(2).

WHO, Regional Office for Europe. 2013. "European Health for All Database", http://www.euro.who.int/en/data-and-evidence/databases/european-health-for-all-database-hfa-db.

Zamagni, S. 1996. "Linee di un disegno istituzionale in campo economico che coniughi sussidiarietà e solidarietà", in Id. (a cura di), *Economia solidale, Piemme*, Casale Monferrato.

Zimmermann, B. 2006. "Pragmatism and the Capability Approach: Challenges in Social Theory and Empirical Research", *European Journal of Social Theory*, Vol 9, Issue 4, pp. 467–484.

The manufacturer's authorised representative in the EU is Springer Nature Customer Service Centre GmbH, Europaplatz 3, 69115 Heidelberg, Germany. If you have any concerns regarding our products, please contact ProductSafety@springernature.com

Printed and bound by CPI Group (UK) Ltd, Croydon, CR0 4YY
30/09/2026
02225576-0014